RIDING RAINBOWS

STEFANIE KERRIDGE

Copyright © Stefanie Kerridge, 2017
Published by I_AM Self-Publishing, 2017.

The right of Stefanie Kerridge to be identified as the Author of the Work has been asserted by her in accordance with the Copyright, Designs and Patents Act 1988.

All rights reserved.

ISBN 978-1-912145-99-7

This book is sold subject to the condition it shall not, by way of trade or otherwise, be circulated in any form or by any means, electronic or otherwise without the publisher's prior consent.

@iamselfpub
www.iamselfpublishing.com

"If you want your children to be intelligent, read them fairy tales. If you want them to be more intelligent, read them more fairy tales."
— Albert Einstein, theoretical physicist

CONTENTS

Anna 7
Mrs Toad 23
Rules of the Chosen 27
At School 31
At the Chosen 50
The Library 68
Through the Tunnels 73
The Program 80
Back in Class 87
Earworms 94
Helping Philip 101
Philip 111
Assembly 118
The Rescue 129
At Philip's house 139
Back in grace 148
Philip's cure 159
More favours 163
Rain 172
Rainbow numbers 177
Success 182
Acknowledgement 190
About The Author 191

ANNA

Anna is running.

Running is so good.

It always helps, and makes her feel free.

What a day she has had. She does not want to think about it anymore.

Just run, run, run. The wind is in her hair and on her face. She dries the salty tears that pop out of her eyes, even though she tries so hard to keep them in.

Anna is eight and a half. She is perfect. Perfect as far as almost everything goes.

She is strong.

She can run fast.

She is a champion on the climbing frame.

The other day she did fifty-one turns on the top bar!

"That is so cool," her best friend Emma had said.

"I wish I could do that. You are so cool. You can run the fastest, spin fifty one times – I am so pathetic!"

"No, you are not," Anna thinks, unhappy about herself as usual.

"She can do everything I want to do. Don't care about spinning, it doesn't make Mummy smile." She loves her mum.

Every day Anna comes home from school and tries hard to make Mummy smile.

First of all, by giving her Mummy her best face.

Next, she tells her all the success stories of the day.

Fifty-one turns on the climbing frame – that should be something! Or having it out with that pathetic little dumpling, Mathilde. And winning!

No. Today again, Mummy has gone straight for the worst:

"How about your spellings? Did you get any?"

"Well, ah – mmh, one."

Anna looks down at the floor.

"Oh dear, Anna, what shall we do with you?" Her mum has that worried look that Anna does not like. Mummy always tries so hard to find a new fun way of helping Anna to remember her spellings. Only yesterday, Mum had looked so excited when she told her: "Anna, I've found this new fun book to practise in. Oh darling, I am so excited. Finally, we will crack this. It is promising. Look, it says, 'Learn 10 spellings a day, The Fun way!' That's what we want."

Anna hates it. The tears well up behind her eyes, followed by a really hot snivelly nose. She just keeps staring at the floorboards hoping for a hole to open up. And – whoops – she could be sucked in; into the nothingness of the under floorboard.

"What is under the ground? Is there any space? And if so, would I fit?"

"Well, sweetheart, I am afraid we just have to keep trying. You know just one thing we can do, and that is:

> Practise.
> Practise.
> Practise."

No point in arguing. Even though they all know, it just doesn't work. No point. That's it. Stupid.

Every afternoon, it is the same old story. If it is not spelling to practise, surely there will be the seven times table, or else: "How about some reading. Anna, I want to help you get a bit faster at reading!"

She knows herself that she is slow, not that she hasn't tried and tried. And Mummy only wants to help.

Her sister Louisa, she is something else!

Only thirteen, she jumped year two, has grade eight in the violin, and is always perfect. Things just come to her with no effort. Not fair.

The attraction of the floorboards becomes even stronger.

"Can you at least listen, Anna, please?"

A great sadness has spread its grey mist all around Anna's head. She feels as if she is in a haze.

There is just so much wrong with her. What was the point in even trying?

Every time Anna looks at her spellings, the letters seem to perform a little dance on the page. They appear to be surrounded by a lovely shine of beautiful colours, like a halo around the moon on a slightly misty night.

Beautiful. Anna loves beautiful things.

But the letters aren't really beautiful. That lovely shine is just a fraud. They are actually hideous, difficult, nasty things!

A scream has welled up in Anna's head: "I hate you!" The shout was aimed at the letters, but Mummy looks shocked at her sudden outburst. "You are very ungrateful, little Anna. We are all really trying so hard to help you." Anna can get so angry so quickly.

"I think we need to get you seen again by that lovely Doctor Powell. I remember, he was so great with Mary when she had that little spell of not eating properly. Mind you, it is very different. She works so hard and is so bright. Why are we still standing in the hall? "

Then Anna sits at her desk, her elbows supporting her head.

She has been watching rainbows dancing around the page as she tries to remember the letters of each word on her spelling list. One of them seems to mock her. Such a tiny little word – but still so nasty! L I G H T. Well, it rhymes with bite, and with fight. Should be easy.

Wow, she thinks of boxers in a ring. Having a fight in the light. And that thing in their mouth was like a thing that you bite. She wears one for playing hockey sometimes. So, what was the word again? She has drifted off a bit.

That is her problem:

Too much imagination!

Not good. Everybody tells her off for daydreaming. She sighs. Has to look at the nasty little word up again.

L I G H T. So small. She has closed her eyes and tried to see the letters, just like her teacher has told her to. She thinks of light. There it goes again. She sees a beautiful light, shining through trees. "No," she tells herself. "You are doing it again. Must stop this. Think of the letters, silly cow!" she nearly shouts at herself.

She has taken her pencil and written out the word, carefully thinking of all the letters:

le i te She sounds them out. *li t*. She looks at what she has written and shakes her head. She remembers now, there was a *g* somewhere.

litg No, it must have an *e*, usually at the end, but *litge* looks funny.

So, it must be *glite*. No, that definitely looks wrong. It has a *t* in the end. so *eglit*. That's it! Must be right. She compares it with her spelling list, feeling very confident. Tick it off?

But – here we go again. Stupid Anna!

That's what Amanda had called her the other day. She said her mum doesn't think it would be such a good idea to invite her round for her eighth birthday party. Clever Amanda, she always gets thirty out of thirty. And that's the top grade ones, not the easy ones like Anna is set by her teacher.

Amanda's mum thinks Anna could be a bad influence. She told Amanda that she was a great disappointment to her parents because she was so, well... just not academic. We don't think poor simple Anna will make it to the 'Upper'.

That's it.

It's so important. Every girl needs to get to the 'Upper', it's such a wonderful school. They all leave with super marks. OK, if the girl is a bit arty or very musical, there are one or two other schools. But you have to pass the entrance test for all of them.

Anna's bones in her left hand, her righting – or is it writing? hand – feel like rubber. The hand just cannot do it. As she thinks about the nasty things that Amanda has said about her, her silly hand instead starts doodling on the edges of her page.

Pretty patterns appear.

Suddenly, they start turning into pictures.

Two snakes. Where are they going? Are they friends, skipping a little funny snake dance?

Out of nowhere, suddenly a hand comes from behind and pulls the paper away.

"I cannot believe it, Anna, you are doing it again. Instead of practising your spellings you just start drawing! " Her mother sounds very upset.

"What am I to do with you? I do not have the time to constantly sit with you to watch that you are working. You are a nightmare." Her mum's voice sounds almost angry now, but also very sad.

Anna has done it again. She always makes Mummy unhappy.

So sad.
She had not wanted to. It just happened.
She felt a lump building up in her throat.
She is stupid.
Nasty.
Dumb.
She jumps up from her chair and runs.
Out of her room and down the stairs.
She opens the front door and keeps running.
"Anna, come back, darling, come on. Try again! Please."
No.
No more.
No point.
She'll never learn.
Running helps.
She feels the wind in her face. Dries some of the tears.
Cools the face.
She does not want to stop.

Her home is in a beautiful location.
Of course.
Mum and Dad work so hard for their children.

There is a famous park behind their house. Full of ancient old trees.

So lovely, her feet take her as if they have a mind of their own.

Thump, thump, thump.

Her heart feels lighter with the rhythm of her legs. Deep breaths.

Yes, she is good at running.

She feels the freshness of the air.

She hears the ducks on the pond, fighting over some old bread that a toddler is dropping into the water. She used to do the same.

Watch the ducks. 'Wucks', she used to call them when she was cute. When Mummy still called her: "My clever little girl!"

There's no more of that these days. She knows that Mum and Dad are just worried about her. They are so patient and try to help as much as they can. It is just that she; well, she is simply not clever enough. She would so much love to impress them for once. Her eyes cloud over as the tears well up again. She leaves the path and starts running across the big meadow, close to the group of trees that she loves to look at so much. They are so old and gnarly. Some of them seem to have faces in their bark. One of them, she thinks, has got arms instead of branches, performing a silent ballet dance.

She passes an ancient oak tree.

"Ouch," she stumbles.

It is as if the tree has stuck out a foot. Deliberately, to make her lose her balance! Just like Nico does in the playground.

"Stupid Anna, look everybody! Can't even run without tripping."

As she falls, she braces herself for the impact.

To her surprise, instead of hurting herself on the hard dried grass, she feels embraced by a delicious softness. A thick layer of dark green moss has cushioned her fall.

She sits up on it and leans her back against the rough bark of the old tree.

As she tries to catch her breath, she starts thinking back on her day.

How disappointing. She is just so useless. What will become of her? She can't play with her little Sylvanians forever. That's when she is at her happiest. They are so cute. She has her auntie's collection. Lots of them. She can play and play and play. She loves it. And, of course, being on the climbing frame, and spinning round and round till she is so dizzy, she feels like she can fly.

It all doesn't count. Really, she is utterly useless.

Her face feels wet. Tears are running down her cheeks.

They form a little stream as they unite with the snot running down below her nose. She hangs her head low and doesn't even bother wiping her face with her T-shirt. Instead, she watches the droplets as they leave her top lip. They form disgusting long strings and then break off and plop, fall down.

One of them lands right on top of a small red toadstool.

Perfectly formed with a red head and a white long stalk. Strange she had not noticed it before.

She looks again. The tear is lying on the top, forming a perfect little droplet.

Is she dreaming?

The droplet works like a magnifying glass. She moves her head closer.

Another dollop leaves her lip and falls.

"Thanks very much," a voice says out of nowhere. "I didn't bring my umbrella. Didn't look like a rainy day. No intention of drowning either."

A very strange little figure appears from underneath the toadstool.

"Who are you?" Anna whispers in a slightly frightened voice.

"Oh, haven't introduced myself. Too busy jumping away from silly old tears. Name is Otto. Read it back to front, or else. Stays the same. Ha ha. Round, just like me."

Anna looks at Otto and realises that the tiny figure is indeed rather round and strange. His head resembles an acorn with its hat on. The body looks like a sturdy round conker. The little man is dressed in bizarre old-fashioned Scottish tartan trousers, called 'plus fours', ending just below his very knobbly knees. A massive big belt is holding them up on his very round waistline. His unusual appearance is finished off with bright red wellington boots on both feet.

"Where have you come from?" Anna says.

"I am always here. Live in this lovely little cottage," he answers, pointing to the toadstool.

And to her surprise, Anna suddenly makes out a very small door, as well as a window, in the stalk. The toadstool's head carries the tiniest of chimneys.

"How come I never saw you and your cottage before?" she asks Otto.

"Well, not everyone can see me and my friends. Only the gifted. And only when they cry tears containing the sorrows of this world," Otto replies.

"I am not gifted! I am stupid. You must be mistaken. But who are the others? Are there more of you?"

"We all belong to the Chosen, the whole lot of us. You'll get to meet them eventually. If you keep to the rules, that is."

"What do you mean?"

"Well, there are always some rules. Need to protect us from the nosey ones, who are not so gifted. Like that stupid girl who nearly stepped on me the other day, girl called Amanda. Her mum was there too. Discussing a party program. Sounded empty-headed. All neat and perfect. No place for invention or ideas. Need those. Boring lot, otherwise."

Anna feels puzzled. Amanda, stupid? Empty-headed? But how, she is so good at school?

"I beg your pardon, Otto, but you are mistaken in thinking that Amanda is stupid. She is so clever at school. Always zero mistakes. Got grades in music too. I can't even read properly. I am the stupid one!"

"Nonsense. You are not stupid. Different. That's all there is. You'll soon see why. Anyhow – are you going to come?"

"Come where?" Anna asks. "Where to?

Warnings start flashing in her mind. "Do not talk to strangers! Never go with someone you don't know." But surely this is not real? No one has warned her of tiny little chestnut men that are small enough to fit into your hand. She almost laughs to herself. Where does he want to take me? Can't be very far. His tiny feet won't take him any distance.

She smiles politely. "You want me to go where?" she asks again.

"Sorry, forgot. It is your first visit. Of course, you don't know how to get there, yet." He points up with his spindly arm. Was it really made out of a tiny twig? "Take some of that teardrop you dropped on my roof onto your finger and put it on your forehead. Then you'll see."

Anna feels intrigued. What can go wrong? After all, it is her own tear. And a toadstool. OK, they are poisonous, but she is not going to stick her finger in her mouth, like a baby.

She does as she is told and rubs some of the tear on her forehead and – feels very strange, very strange indeed!

Colours fill the air around her. A rainbow, she thinks. But it hasn't rained? It is now surrounding her completely now, like a whirlpool in an angry river. Down, down it spins.

Faster and faster.

"Weee...eee- so much fun!!"

She is actually riding the rainbow spiral. Better than Alton Towers, she imagines. But she has never been, her parents don't approve.

She is really enjoying this.

Then the colours fade, and with a soft 'plop', she lands on her bottom.

She looks up. Otto is smiling at her. The little chestnut man suddenly appears taller than Anna. Weird!

He waves one of his twiggly arms and invites her to follow him.

She looks around. This is such a strange place she's in now. A thick jungle of green stems surrounds the path they are following. "Looks like massive tall grass!" Weird.

The grass can't have grown so fast. Never. It is taller than she is. She suddenly realises: "I have shrunk!"

She is so tiny now that every grass blade is the size of a small tree. She looks up. The round seed head of a dandelion is towering above her. A gentle breeze shakes some of the white parachute shaped seeds off and they float above her head. They are so massive, Anna feels that if she could grab one, she could hold on and fly away with it. That would be really great fun.

But she decides to follow this funny little Otto instead. Together they follow the path through the tall grass. When they stop they look at a strange large hollow that has formed below the roots of the old oak tree.

She had never noticed it before. It just looked like any of those dark little spaces that are formed at the bottom of many trees. "Wow!" Her jaw drops as she realises it to be a mysterious huge airy space that has been formed by the roots of the ancient gnarly tree. A soft glow gently shines from deep inside her.

"What is this?" Anna asks her new companion.

"It is the hollow, a cave inside the old oak.

This is our winter world. When it gets too cold for living inside a toadstool. It is also the place where our boss lives."

"Who is your boss?"

Otto is not a man of many words. He replies with a strong Scottish drawl: "Oh, just old Toady. She is so wise. She always knows what is best for all of us. Have to introduce you. She'll tell you the rules."

He knocks politely on the root just below the sign.

MRS TOAD

"Who is there?" A full but croaky voice comes from the depths of the hollow.

"It's me, Otto and Anna."

"Oh good, has she finally found her way here? Been waiting for ages! Come on in, my friends."

It seems completely normal to Anna that both Otto and Mrs Toad already know her name.

As she is stepping closer, she is surprised how spacious and lovely the hollow looks. In the middle of the big room is a very old-fashioned stove. It has a glass front that allows the flames to spread their soft, flickering light around the walls, which are formed by the strong old roots.

Several smaller rooms lead off this main room. Like in an old-fashioned kitchen, the main room is spanned by numerous lines, and a variety of mushrooms and herbs hang from them, drying in the warmth of the oven.

Old Toady stands bent over a chunky kitchen table, busy tying threads around bundles of herbs. She is wearing a polka dot apron tied in a very big bow behind her back. Like Anna's beloved granny, she is a bit plump, which just makes her warty face look even friendlier. Her looks are finished off with a huge pair of pointed sunglasses.

"Preparing for the winter," she says with a friendly smile across her face. "Going to have quite a few people staying here when it comes to the cold season. But let me welcome our new friend first."

She gives Anna a big hug and kisses her on both cheeks.

Anna had always thought frogs and toads had cold and wet skin.

To her surprise, Toady's lips felt dry, soft and almost warm on her cheeks.

Toady giggles: "Thinking that I should turn into a princess, if you kiss me back? Better not! Useless creatures, princes and princesses. Any old toad, or even frog, is far more useful."

Anna grins back, this old toad seems nice.

"So, tell me Anna, what brings you here today?"

Anna tells her about her awful day, of running out of the house, landing on the soft, inviting moss cushion and of finally meeting Otto.

"Well, well," Toady looks at Anna's face with a very caring smile. "Looks like you deserve to be one of the Chosen, the privileged."

"Otto has mentioned something similar to that before, but I don't quite understand, because I am naturally stupid. I can't really read, write, and remember my simplest times tables. I mix up a lot of things and am permanently getting into muddles. So why would I be priliveged, sorry, perliveged?" With a sigh, she says: "There you are, you see. Stupid Anna."

"Oh you poor thing. No, you are not. Stupid, that is. You'll soon learn that you are so very wrong in what you perceive to be the truth about yourself. We'll make you truly one of us. But first, I have to introduce you to our rules. Sorry about that. But it is important. We must make sure that we protect ourselves."

She pulls out a piece of paper.

Rules of the Chosen

In the Park

1. Do **not** lend your tears to A n y o n e!

2. Never tell any of the Empty-headed about the Chosen!

3. Never forget the reason for coming to the Chosen!

In a clear voice, she reads the three rules slowly to Anna.

"If you are happy to oblige and agree to the above rules, you are welcome to become a member of the Chosen."

Anna nods, the rules sound OK. She doesn't understand quite why she should not share her tears. What a strange thing, she's never had any opportunity for that anyway. Who would want her tears?

As if she was able to read her mind, Mrs Toad explains:

"It is all about self-protection. If we share a tear or two, we'll get the wrong kind of people down to us. They would never understand us. They would just tell each other about strange ideas in strange people's heads and that it was all total rubbish.

"They'll talk about everything being just a pile of acorns, conkers, leaves, twigs and so on. They cannot see what you see. They are just not naturally gifted."

"Wow, you really think I am special? Gifted? Gifted means going to the 'Upper'! Will I go there?"

"Don't be silly. This is not what gifted means. Except in the 'Empty-headeds' minds.

To us, gifted means being open, able to see things from different angles, being unusual, full of ideas. That is the reason you find it so hard to learn the way they teach you. It is them who can't think of something better. Forget the 'Upper'. It is a perfectly alright place for some, but you are far too special for that. We'll find a better place for you, eventually. First, you'll have a bit of learning to do."

"But, eh, I can't really learn too well," Anna explains politely in a quiet embarrassed voice, feeling the heat as her cheeks blush to a strong crimson red. She does not want to offend this lovely lady, but she also doesn't want to make her unhappy, like she always does with Mummy.

"Oh, Mummy!!" she suddenly thinks.

"I must have been away for ages! My mum will be worried," she quickly says to Otto and Mrs Toad.

The latter beams her heartwarming smile at Anna and explains that they are all tiny down here, so tiny that it takes such a long spiral ride to get to them. Because of that, time is also really quite short compared with big people's time. So Anna needn't worry about having been away for long. In fact, what she thought were hours, were only a few minutes in real time.

Anna feels relieved. On the one hand she would love to spend more time with Otto and Mrs Toad, but on the other hand she does not want to upset her mum anymore.

Otto, who has been busy helping Mrs Toad with the bundling of the herbs, senses her unrest.

He holds out one of his twiggy arms and invites Anna:

"Aye, time for this young lassie to return home."

Mrs Toad nods in agreement. She reaches up to one of the lines above her head and pulls off a little herb bundle and explains: "Take these herbs with you. Put them under your pillow at night. They'll help you to dream the right dreams. The right dreams help us to have a better day. Take care now, my love. I'll see you soon."

After a little hug, Anna bids farewell and is led out of the hollow by Otto. He leads her back to the moss cushion.

"Just sit down here. To get back you have to use your imagination. Just think of a lovely rainbow formed by the sun shining through your teardrop. You'll get a lift up the spiral with that. When you want to return, you know what to do?"

"Yes, I think so. Do I cry tears containing the sorrows of the world onto your cottage roof and then rub a bit onto my forehead?" she asks.

"Aye, that is correct. As long as you don't flood my wee hus out. You'll be alright." He laughs at her in his jolly, friendly way.

Anna shakes hands with the little guy. She doesn't want to hug or kiss him because he is so round, she fears she wouldn't reach.

Anna closes her eyes and sure enough, she sees the wonderful colours of a rainbow shining like a magical light through a teardrop and – whoosh – she spirals back to the place below the old oak tree in the park.

She can still just make out a tiny arm waving to her from below the toadstool. It is Otto's, her tiny new friend's, a chestnut man's hand.

AT SCHOOL

Anna finds it hard to get up in the morning.

As she stretches first her arms, then her legs, one by one... Oh, so good... She finds she does not want to say goodbye to the last lovely dream that she just had. She can still see some of the things in her mind's eye.

A funny looking toad wearing very funky glasses; acorns and chestnuts held together by bits of twig, forming figures like little people dressed in Scottish clothes; mushrooms on strings, leaves and herbs...

"Hold on," Anna says, as she tries to cling on to some of the images as they burst away from her vision, like soap bubbles when you touch them.

"Hold on, was it only a dream?"

Quickly she sticks her left hand under her pillow.

"Yes!" Anna shouts as she feels the brittle dry herbs given to her by Mrs Toad the previous day. "Yes, it's true."

She takes the precious herbs out and hides them in the left-hand drawer of her small writing desk. There they lie amongst her other treasures – marbles with lovely patterns, a little figure from a 'Kinder Surprise' egg, almost complete, two magnets in the shape of mice, holding on to each other because of the magnetic attraction. Great fun. Turn them the other way and they chase each other!

She has lots more stuff in that drawer; well away from Mrs Davids, the cleaner.

She is a rather lovely lady who often looks after Anna and her sister when Mummy is too busy at work. But she does not understand why some things are important to Anna. They look like rubbish to her.

Anna definitively does not want to risk losing the lovely herbs.

Lovely dreams. Unlike many nights when she wakes up clammy with sweat, her fists tight after some kind of fight. Or worse, a chase where her legs feel like they weigh a ton and she cannot run.

No, last night had been so nice. She'd love to continue sleeping.

"Anna, get a move on! Seven forty-five!" That's Dad's voice. He doesn't hang around in the morning.

The worst thing is to make him late.

It is his job to take the girls to school.

With a deep sigh, Anna slowly puts on her clothes. Her thoughts are still miles away. Well, not miles. To be precise, they are in the park underneath an old oak tree, in front of a lovely toadstool cottage.

Wasn't there a swing seat attached to the roof? She can imagine sitting in it and gently pushing herself, higher and higher against the blue sky.

"I wish I could fly," she thinks as she finally makes her way downstairs to the kitchen.

She is greeted by the violent laughter of her sister.

"Look, dad, look what she's done this time! Look. Shirt on top of her jumper. That beats shoes on the wrong foot! Ha ha ha..." Her sister can barely stop giggling, always prim and proper.

"Oh, dear, stupid me again." She is trying not to get upset as she takes her shirt and jumper off and puts them back on in the right order.

She looks up as she hears her dad's strict voice: "Anna, breakfast. Come on, girl, we don't have all day."

"Dad, does the world always turn round the same way?"

"Now, what a silly question is that then, Anna? There'd be no daylight next day if it didn't."

"But will it always be like that? Who says?"

"Eat your cereals. Special ones for you. We are trying you with lots of that omega three stuff now. Don't use the dairy milk. You have your own soya one. Hope it helps," he adds mumbling.

He is thinking about his two girls. They are so different! Just like chalk and cheese. He knows he gets too impatient with poor little Anna sometimes. He just can't understand why things are so hard for her and so easy for Louisa. You only had to tell her things once and –whoops – learned! Never to be forgotten. He sighs. They had been so spoilt with their firstborn. But Anna... he is quite worried about her. They have tried so many things, bought every little learning book or toy they could get to help her along. Now, when he watched her come down with her clothes on the wrong way round, he just... well he really doesn't get it. She does not look stupid. What is going on?

"Seatbelts and off," he says when the three of them are finally in the car. "Anna, let's just check on your seven times table again. What does 4x7 make?

She thinks hard. She knows 2x7 =14. So 41 add on 7 = 48, or 84.

"Eighty-four," she says, knowing it does not quite sound right. "No, 48," she corrects herself.

"Come on Anna, are you having me on? 48 is not in the sevens at all. Think about it. Have you not got any idea how big it roughly should be? Start at 2 sevens. Go on!!"

He is starting to show his impatience. Anna can see she is doing really badly again. This time it is dad she is making sad. Or angry? She can see from the back of his neck that he is clenching his teeth. It makes his chin look very square.

"Still waiting!"

Anna plops back to the stupid old tables: "2 sevens fourteen." She whispers.

"Louder!"

"Two sevens are fourteen," she is just able to squeeze the sound out, as something is choking her. Was it the right way round this time?

"Well, thank the Lord. For once! My daughter knows the right answer. Now work it out, what is 14 + 7?"

"Don't know, dad. Knew it tomorrow. But forgotten." She works out quietly in her head: '1 add 7, eight, add 7, twelve.'

"Dad. Twelve." She knows it does not sound good, it must be the other way round. "Twenty one, Dad, I mean."

"Next time, a bit more prompt. Takes you too long, sweetie. You must practise more."

Her sister is giggling again: "Dad, did you not hear what she said? She said..." she is laughing too much now she can barely speak. "She said, haha, she said 'knew it tomorrow', hahaha."

Anna shoots her a glance that could have easily killed her if that was possible.

"I mean yesterday. Honest. Dad. I knew it yesterday. But I forget it all the time!" She is shouting now.

"Leave me alone!" She screams at her sister. "Just leave me alone."

"Now, Anna, calm down. Your sister and I, we are both trying to help you. We all know you find it difficult. But you need to practise. Never mind. Daddy loves you anyway. Just keep trying."

She can tell from his face, even though he is driving, that he is quite sick of her stupidity.

What had Mrs Toad said? That she was gifted? She is now giggling.

"Anna, what is so funny? Are you having me on? Are you even trying?"

"I feel gifted," she just comes out with it, out of the blue in a slightly shaky voice. She just wants to test this. You never know. Adults.

Mind you, exceptions. Mrs Toad had seemed such an intelligent lady, or rather toad.

"Oh my poor darling," Dad finds it hard to keep his eyes focused on the road ahead. "You have lots of good things. You are really good at running. That's something. You probably got that from me. But the real thing, school and stuff, you find that very difficult.

I wonder if we are doing the right thing for you. Mum and I have just heard of this special school. One where the children improve so well. The only thing is that you would have to stay during the week. But that could be fun, hey Anna? They encourage sports. Don't get it wrong, sweetheart, nothing is decided yet. It is very expensive..." His voice fades out.

By the time they arrive at her school, Anna feels really 'great'. Being called stupid at school is bad enough, but getting the same at home, first thing in the morning, even before breakfast – that is almost too much to bear. Her stomach feels like it's been filled with bricks.

"Staying away, special school," her dad's words echo in her head.

On her way across the playground, she keeps her head down. She kicks up little stones with her feet. Well, new shoes. How much she had been looking forward to showing them off to Emma. It's not very often a girl likes her school shoes. But these, wow, she never thought she could get nice ones like that. But now, she thinks: "Does it really matter what my shoes look like?"

Oh dear, there is Amanda. It is not fair. She is always so pretty. Just so coordinated, not a hair out of place.

"I passed my next piano grade! Mummy and I think I am almost certainly going to get a scholarship for the 'Upper'.

Oh, sorry, didn't upset you, did I? Forgot for a moment that you find it hard. It just comes to me, you know. Just comes with no effort. Did you ever even try to learn an instrument?" She does not look at all sorry about anything. Rather, she smiles a smug grin at Anna, very full of herself.

Anna looks up at the other girl. Her throat is getting very tight and seems to be filling with a bitter substance.

"Cow, bitch, hate you," she thinks. An enormous hot wave of extreme anger fills her head. And suddenly out of the blue, without warning and knowing what is coming over her, she charges at her opponent and – finds herself biting into Amanda's back!

Amanda, in her unexpected shock, screams excruciatingly.

In no time at all, lots of kids gather around to watch.

Anna feels a heavy hand pulling her off the other girl. The hand belongs to Mr Samuel, one of the nice teachers. He is a bit like she would love her dad to be – quite laidback and relaxed. When he was her form teacher, he used to reassure her: "Don't worry, Anna, just keep trying. If you give it your best, you'll get there eventually."

But not now. This is different. No more nice teacher. Anna finds him looking at her in a very changed way. He looks almost disgusted.

He snarls at her: "Well, I can't believe it. That is one step too far, young lady. This is horrid. I am afraid I will have to send you straight away to Mrs Bingfield's office. Poor little Amanda. That was totally unprovoked and evil. I never thought of you as being in that category. So shocking. And biting, imagine – biting!"

He turns away from her. "Are you alright, Amanda? Are you injured? Better go to the sick bay. A bite is something nasty, better get it seen to. Emma, will you be so kind and take her there?"

Anna's head hangs even lower now. She does not want to meet the eyes of anyone, she's so ashamed. The weirdest thing is that biting into Amanda's back had actually felt quite good, for a moment anyway. She must be strange. Maybe Mummy is right, maybe she should go and have another session with Dr Powell. She doesn't really like him, he has those white bits in the corners of his mouth, yuck!

But she now has to make herself go to Mrs Bingfield's office and she is dreading it. She is quite frightened of Mrs Bingfield. Such a big lady, she seems to tower over the children. Her head looks as if it is miles up. And with that strange false smile attached to it, she could easily be a secret witch. Anna's feet seem to be glued to the ground.

Mr Samuel's voice drones into her already buzzing ears: "Did you not hear what I said? Go and see Mrs Bingfield, now, I mean. If I have to drag you there personally, you'll be in even bigger trouble then you already are."

She has never heard Mr Samuel sound like this before.

She lifts her head a tiny bit, and in a desperate attempt to avoid going to the head mistress' office, pleads: "I am so sorry. Sir. I did not mean to. I don't know what came over me. Please Sir, can I, please nnnot ggo to Mrs Bingfield's, pppplease."

She is stuttering. Big rivers of salty tears are streaming down her face now. What has she done?

"You are disappointing me even further, Anna. What you have done is inexcusable. And now,

now you don't even stand up to face the music. That is just so... I don't even have the words for it. Cowardly, I suppose." There is no niceness at all in his look. "Go now, last warning." His eyes look petrifying. His whole face has taken on the colour of a beetroot.

What she has done is awful. She knows that she is in deep trouble.

Anna cannot really remember anything she said in Mrs Bingfield's office later, when she is returning to her classroom.

All she remembers is that she cried and cried, and that Mrs Bingfield had said something about warning her. Unacceptable behaviour.

Not in her school.

That her parents would have to be informed, and so on. She tried not to think of the mega trouble there would be at home. Violent, that's what the head teacher had called it.

Violent.

No more playtime with the others. Review in a month's time. Set work in the library. She did not mind so much. No more friends now, anyway. Again, she feels a little cry of despair well up. But her parents? A daughter stupid and violent too, oh no.

The large teacher rises from her seat. She tells Anna that the school cannot trust her anymore. So she'll have to walk her back to class. That is just so scary. She pushes Anna virtually out of her office. Her golden bangles make a metallic sound behind the back of Anna's neck, like the handcuffs of a policewoman marching her along the corridor. She opens the classroom door, and without a further word, turns round to walk back to her office.

Anna enters the classroom.

Immediately, everyone falls silent and stares at her. Her seat is almost right at the back. She normally likes it there. It gives her more opportunity to hide. But now she feels all eyes fixed on her as she makes a long journey through the room.

Amanda is sitting next to Isabel. They both look at each other, then at her, then back at each other in a very arrogant way. Apart from her eyes being a little bit red, Amanda is back to her usual perfect self again, showing a triumphant little curve to the corner of her mouth.

After what seems like ages, with all eyes following her to her desk, she quietly glides onto her chair next to Emma. At least she has one friend. She turns a sideways glance, trying to form a little grin in her direction. But Emma suddenly appears awfully busy with her Maths set work as she turns her head quickly away from Anna.

"Stop that smug look of yours, Anna! We have, of course, all heard about that terrible attack of yours in the playground. So shocking! How can anyone be so viciously violent to poor Amanda darling. Amanda who has never done anything nasty to anyone."

Her form teacher breathes a deep sigh.

"Now, for goodness sake, take out your Maths and get going. You are so far behind anyway."

Anna looks at her work. It is supposed to be set at her level. Some of the other children are already into long divisions and difficult stuff like that. She is still doing simple multiplications. That awful seven and eight times table. She just can't do it!

She suddenly feels some hot air on her neck and smells the slightly foul breath of her teacher.

Normally, they all joke about it. "Imagine. She has breath like a field full of dung, her husband... oh no! They giggle." And so on. Normally, that is. Now, she is sure that nobody will joke with her ever again.

She is out.

Not cool.

"How much have you done so far? Well, by the looks of it, nothing at all. I just can't believe it. Young lady, I'll record the time you started and finished on here. Then your parents can see exactly how little you have done. They need to realise how slow and lazy you are, my dear."

"Wow, even more trouble is building up! It started all wrong this morning. Then it carried on in the same way. What next?" The upset girl allows her thoughts to wander back, back to the tree in the park, the hollow and its occupants. She can't wait to be able to return...

At lunch she sits with kids who are not from her class. None of the usual crowd is willing to be seen beside her. She feels very lonely.

In the middle of trying to swallow her food, which just seems to be too dry, no matter how much she chews it, she suddenly hears the voice of a boy next to her.

"Hear you're in trouble. Always the same with me. Get carried away." He smiles at her. "Not so keen on my pud. You have it." He pushes his bowl of fruit salad over to her.

"Thanks. That's cool. Why are you nice to me?" She suddenly looks at him suspiciously.

She doesn't really know him, just heard of him. He is known as 'Loony', as he is always up for something crazy. Always chasing around, never sits still, even in class or assembly. He is in the year above, but she knows he too is one of the 'not so clever' ones. The only thing he is really good at is at playing 'practical jokes'.

Most kids are a bit scared of him. He gets too easily 'overexcited', or to tell the truth, he gets quite violent.

He is a very tall boy. His hair falls down into his face in what would normally be described as beautiful curls, if they weren't so disgustingly greasy. His fingernails are long too, and very black.

"Yuck," she thinks. She feels strange, when she looks at him. On the one side, he is revolting her, on the other side...

Like her, he is very impressive in the playground. Running away from trouble is his greatest strength.

Anna has heard some of the girls secretly giggling when he's been around, because underneath all of the scruffiness he is actually quite 'cool', as they would put it. Tall and slim with big hazel coloured eyes, Anna suddenly realises that she likes looking at him.

"Hey, could say something instead of staring. Are you here or miles away? Eat!"

With a little jerk Anna comes back to the reality of the dining hall. Suddenly, all the voices around her appear to be turned on full volume.

"Sorry, had such a tough morning," Anna says as she picks up the spoon to shovel the bits of sweet fruit up.

"I am dreading the rest of the day, especially when I get back home. Gonna be told off like mad," she adds with a deep sigh. "Bound to be grounded, or so. Just means work, work, work. Really horrible! I don't mind working if it would get me somewhere. But to be honest, it is just a complete waste of time. Too thick. Can't read. Can't write. Can't do tables. My spelling is the worst." She looks very upset, but also very pretty, Philip thinks.

He understands very well what she is going through. "Been there lots of times. To hell with it all. You know the latest threat? They might put me down a year. Can you imagine that? I am one of the tallest anyway. My dad made up a soppy story. Me having been ill and so on. Ha. Everyone knows. Just played truant! But, I tell you – not gonna have that. Rather run away."

Anna shudders. She is thinking back to her dad mentioning boarding school. 'Do teachers or parents ever understand?' she is wondering. If you feel bad because you're rubbish, all you want is a hug from them and to be told that all be fine in the end. Not them piling on more rubbish.

The dinner lady is coming over to them. They've been sitting there for absolute ages!

"Hey guys, are you going to stay the night or are you going to clear away your junk? You are nearly the last ones out." She gives the table a wipe with her very smelly grey cloth that stinks like a wet rat.

"Hate the cloth stink. Never washes it out," Anna crumbles up her nose as they are tidying there stuff away.

"Yeah – we're only kids you know. They can get away with it."

They both part at the playground. Wouldn't be cool to be seen together. They both know, so no words are needed. Only a nod and a 'see ye' as they go their own ways.

Anna saunters over towards Emma and some other girls. As she approaches, they immediately fall silent.

"Hey, what's wrong, do I smell?"

They look at each other and then turn away from her. Emma hesitates a moment. She really is a nice girl but she too turns away to join the others, almost whispering, "Sorry," as she does so.

Anna feels as if she is an alien on a little island surrounded by a sea of children moving around,

having fun,

lots of noise,

screams of joy,

laughter,

chatting,

giggling.

It is only she who is alone. She has never ever felt like this before. Horrible.

With a sudden fright she remembers she is not even supposed to be here at all! The library! She drags her new shoes over the tarmac as she slowly makes her way there.

Miss James is in charge. She has been expecting her: "Your work is set out for you. Quite a bit to do. You are very late. Have you been secretly sneaking out to the playground?"

Anna shakes her head. "Sorry, Miss. No. Had a few problems with my tummy. Spent ages on the loo."

"So, really? Come on, sit down and get started," says the older teacher impatiently, she has heard the tummy excuse loads of times before.

She looks at Anna's Maths and makes a funny 'ta ta ta' clicking noise with her tongue: "You certainly are working at a very low level, dear, dear..."

'Finally, saved by the bell,' Anna thinks when playtime is over. Normally, she would make it last as long as possible, quickly dashing to the furthest corner of the playground, pretending she didn't hear the bell.

But not now.

She barely notices what is going on in class. Even though this subject is her favourite: Art. Her pieces usually get some praise. She is clever with colours and draws really well.

Today, she is even rubbish at that. It is some wishy-washy picture in the end. And on top of everything else, it gets messed up when Mathilda 'accidently' pushes her murky water jar over as she passes her table, spilling its contents all over the painting.

There's no telling off from the teacher for Mathilda. Even though it was quite obvious that it was not totally accidental.

"So – ry," she stretches the word in a way that shows she does not mean it.

Anna is digging her fingernails into her closed palms. She is desperately trying not to get furious.

Anna has had enough trouble for the day, more than she needs.

As soon as she sits in the back of her mum's four-wheel drive car after school, she knows mum has been informed by the school about her evil deed.

Mum always gives a lift to three other children on Thursdays, as well as collecting her. Car sharing. Saves the environment and also makes it easier for working parents.

Anna knows just from her mum's face and the way she says: "Seatbelt, Anna," in a very sharp, clipped voice. Cold, like steel. There's no, "Hi, darling", or such.

She smiles briefly at the other three – all carefully selected children from nice families. Mum pretends as if nothing has happened. She is good at pretending. One does not want to have a scene in front of others.

"Well, Anna, I think we need to have a little chat, the two of us," she says as soon as they arrive home.

"Here we go," Anna feels what is coming.

To her surprise, her mum does not say anything for a while. She just gives her a long strange look.

Then she simply asks: "Why? Anna, why?"

Anna looks down at her feet and her ears make a strange ringing noise.

"Don't know," she presses out. "Just felt sooo angry."

"We need to talk about this with your father. This is just too much. You know, we can probably cope with you not doing well at school, but a daughter turning vicious and nasty... We cannot and we will not understand or support this. I will decide tonight, together with Dad, what we will do with you. Of course, you need to be punished, quite severely. To give you a message to never, and I say n e v e r, to do anything like that again!"

After a very deep breath, she looks at her little girl in a very disappointed way and tells her: "Now, go and do your homework and the extra spellings. And no dreaming or doodling, you hear me!

AT THE CHOSEN

Anna is sitting at her desk, really trying harder than ever to concentrate on her work.

She has to draw the water cycle. This is something she can do. She happily follows the journey of the tiny water droplet through rivers, clouds and the sea.

It reminds her of her journey down the spiral to Mrs Toad's.

She opens the drawer of her desk. Yes, the little bundle of herbs are still there. She closes her eyes as she takes in the beautiful scent. She is instantly reminded of the cosines in the hollow. The warm glow of the stove, Mrs Toad's inviting smile. She feels such an enormous longing for her new friends, she can't bear to sit any longer at her desk.

She pushes back her chair, jumps up and shouts down to her mum: "Have to do my running training, Mummy. Preparing for the inter-school challenge. Finished with the homework. Do the spellings after. Promise!"

She does not give her mum a chance to object. She is so fast out of the door.

Feeling the wind around her head is so good. It clears a lot of trouble from her mind already. However, she does not find it difficult at all when she arrives at the old oak tree to cry a tear or two. The thought of being in Mrs Bingfield's office is enough to cause a tidal wave! Added to that, the loss of her friendship with Emma and the trouble with Amanda sets her off totally.

She aims a drop onto the roof of the toadstool cottage, careful not to let the whole flood drown out the garden. She then takes the tear and gently rubs it onto her forehead. She can barely believe the speed with which the magic works. Wow! For the first time today, she feels really great as she is circling down the rainbow spiral into the hidden world of the Chosen!

As expected, her landing is cushioned by the softness of the fresh moss. Slightly dizzy she looks around to find her friend Otto. She can't see him. She knocks on the little cottage door. No answer.

"Oh no, what shall I do now?" She looks around. It is a bit scary. Should she try and find her way to the tree with the hollow on her own? The spears of grass, which look very short when she is her normal size, form a dense woodland around Otto's garden. She is worried she might lose her way. She hesitates. Maybe she'd better sit down and wait for a bit. There is a choice. She can use Otto's little bench seat right next to the front door of the toadstool, or should she try that swing she found so tempting before? Would he mind? She decides that it will be OK to have a go on the swing.

She loves it. The long rope is made of a strange white material.

A tiny bit sticky.

'Spider thread!' she suddenly realises.

Not unpleasant to touch.

A small piece of bark forms the comfortable seat on which she now climbs. Anna pushes herself with one foot off the ground and manages to get the swing into motion. It is the best one she's been on, ever. It's so weightless, like a flight. She moves to and fro, underneath the toadstool head. She puts her head back and looks up. The roof of Otto's cottage looks beautiful against the milky blue of the sky, as it swings in and out of her view.

Was it her imagination, or did she just get the glimpse of a spider waving at her from the roof? She slows down, but the friendly looking eight-legged creature has disappeared.

Instead, she hears a very loud trampling sound, similar to the 'clip clop' of a horse's hooves.

It is coming closer. She slows her swing to a halt and looks around, slightly worried, when a large shadow falls over her.

She turns around and gets a fright looking up at a huge black face that is looking down at her with giant eyes. She realises that it is an enormous ant smiling down at her.

She looks up and discovers her friend Otto sitting astride on it, his round figure resembling a really funny knight in armour on his horse.

"Oh, hello, Anna!" he greets her. "Been swinging a long time? Meet my pal Oskar," he points to the ant as he rolls down its back.

"He's been so nice as to take me on a visit to my cousin's. He lives underneath the beech hedge. Too far for my poor wee legs to carry my handsome self. Should see his place, like a mansion. Not like my wee hus. He has a whole cluster of mushrooms. A room in each. Never shows off, decent lad. Anyway, how are you?"

"Oh Otto, I have had such a nasty day today. But I am so glad to be here again. That swing of yours made me feel so good, as if I was flying. Really cool. I did not know you could ride on ants! Many kids I know just trample on them. Just for fun." She catches sight of Oskar's face, which had gone completely pale, and realises what she has just said.

"Oskar, I am so sorry. What a careless, awful thing of me to say in your company. I really am so sorry. Please forgive me. Personally, I would never do anything like that at all." She gets quite red in her face and stutters: "Except, ... today, I, I did something so horrible. I would never have thought I'd do that either. I, oh I still can't believe it myself, I... bit a girl!! Imagine. Biting another person!

Now you probably don't like me anymore, just like my friends." She looks down at the ground.

Otto looks at her in a serious but not unfriendly way. He asks: "Did you know what you were doing.

I mean did you really want to hurt this other person or did it just come over you?"

Anna nods in surprise, lifting her flushed face slightly.

"Did you feel a sudden heat and see some red colour around you?"

Again Anna nods her head, still feeling very embarrassed.

"That, Anna, was an encounter with the dangerous Queen of Fury. She throws her red hot veil over people and makes them her slaves."

Anna looks at him in surprise. That was exactly what it had felt like. All red around her, as if some magic powers had overcome her, she had sunk her teeth into the back of the other girl.

"This is our worst enemy, Anna. The 'Empty-Headed' can never see or feel the Queen coming. Causes a lot of problems in our world. But the Chosen, the gifted, can learn to see her coming. So usually we manage to protect ourselves. You should be able to see her coming for you. Mind you, there is still a lot of learning left for you."

He turns round to Oskar. "Have to go and fetch your reward for taking me on the ride. I know you have more jobs to go to. Won't keep you too long, hang on a sec." With that he waddles in his funny way to his cottage.

Anna looks back at Oskar. She still feels bad about what she has said, but he is smiling at her.

"Don't worry, Anna. I can see you for who you are. I know you would not hurt me or my relations. In fact, I think you will become a kind protector of the ant transport community. You can help us a lot. Tell as many as possible of those ignorant children how important we are! Most of them just don't know what they are doing. They are not all bad."

Anna gladly promises him that she will be on the forefront of the ant protection league from now on.

They both shake hands over this.

Then Oskar does something rather strange. Like a cat cleaning itself, he wipes his forearms a few times over his head. Next, he picks up a small leaf from the undergrowth and wipes the sticky paste he has collected from his arms onto it.

"Take this cream, Anna. Take it back with you. It is an anti-anger cream we produce. To you and me it smells really nice, but that horrible wicked Queen can't stand it. So, if you feel that red heat approaching you again, quickly apply a small amount onto your earlobes before the veil is thrown over you. You will instantly notice the ringing in your ears stops and that you are cooling down. The veil will disappear."

Anna can't believe the great kindness of these new friends. She stands on her tiptoes and gives the ant a big hug.

"Thank you, Oskar," she says gladly.

At that moment, Otto comes back from his cottage whistling a happy tune. He carries a small glass with a clear liquid in it in his twiggy hands.

"Ah, nice, thanks. Nectar water. So refreshing," Oscar drowns the liquid quickly.

"Well, it's the least I can give my friend for carrying me around. I know, I'm not the lightest fella. Wee bit on the round side, haha. Well, thank you so much! Good job."

The ant bids them farewell. He is in a hurry with another assignment to go to by the rhododendron bushes at the other end of the park. Someone needs a taxi to visit a sick relation.

Anna folds her leaf over very carefully before she puts it in the back pocket of her jeans.

Otto knew the ant would give her the protective cream. He is glad for Anna and grins at her, indicating that she should follow him once again to the hollow. They politely knock before they hear Mrs Toad call out.

"Is that you, Otto, my dear?"

"Aye, it certainly is and I brought our wee friend Anna with me."

"Oh, nice, just come in the two of you."

Anna immediately feels the warm wave of kindness floating towards her from the old toad.

"And how are you today, my lovely? Oh, can I detect a little troubled look in your eyes?"

Anna gives her a surprised little nod. She has always been so good at acting and hiding her true feelings. How did Mrs Toad guess?

"Tell old Toady all your worries, dear. Then let's find some magic."

She tells her about the events of the day. The nastiness she had experienced as well as the horrible thing she had done.

"I see. You have had some intense contact with the red hot veil and my strongest enemy, the Queen of Fury. That is dangerous and very bad luck. She is such a devious creature. She makes everyone think it was you who was bad. She is very clever.

Do you know, Anna, she needs other people to do nasty deeds and have evil thoughts. She lives off that. It's her food and the air she breathes. She has even caused wars between countries!"

She looks at Anna through her funky sunglasses with a deep worry frown between her eyes. "Listen. This is terribly important: you need to protect yourself from her!"

"I got some protective cream from Oskar, the ant," Anna reassures her.

"Yes, that is superb. But it might not always do the trick. The wicked Queen has so many disguises. You need to learn to recognise the early signs of her approaching. Can you remember what you felt, and how it was before she suddenly threw her veil over you?"

"I remember being already quite annoyed about my Dad and my sister. I tried to tell my Dad that I was not totally useless. That I was, eh hem, like you told me, gifted."

Her voice fades and she is blushing with embarrassment. "You and Otto had told me I was. So I tried, thinking that maybe he would start believing in me. But, no, of course not. I can't do clever things. Only run or draw. Does not count." Tears are starting to well up in her eyes again.

"Now, now," the soothing voice of Mrs Toad gently says. "Listen, we will start you on our special learning program very soon. As soon as we have a space after the last kid, a nice young boy. He is nearly there. Fulfilled all the relevant criteria pretty fast. Just a day or two. In the meantime, use the cream. It will help you."

Otto grins at both of them. " Jolly nice stuff anyway. I admit, like using it sometimes. Great polish for my conker."

"Typical Otto, thinks of his looks as usual," Toady laughs.

"Anna, I think you did very well trying to convince your dad. But until you believe 100 percent in yourself, you'll find it hard to convince others."

"Mrs Toad, you are so wise. May be you can give me advice. I'll have to sit down with my Mum and Dad later. What should I say to them?"

Toady's warty face crinkles in deep thought before she replies:

"Tell them the truth. How much it hurts you when people mock or criticise you. Ask them to help you to fight the anger when it comes. They are very nice people, they love you. It makes them feel better, if they can help you. Explain to them that you actually are trying hard, that you are not stupid, but find it hard to remember certain things that are unfortunately important to them and the teachers at school."

Anna is trying to take the advice in, but how can she convince her parents?

"Anyway, Anna, I hear that you are fantastic at acting?"

Anna blushes. "I wouldn't say fantastic, but I love it. Who told you that?"

The old toad grins her extremely broad smile as she answers:

"You are not the only one who comes here, you know? There are quite a nice few of you lot. You'll find out in due course, they all do. It is a great network amongst the Chosen, you'll see. A group of secret friends."

"Wow, cool. Friends? Really? That would be so nice."

"Yes," you need to be a bit patient. And careful, stick to the rules! That is very important. Do not give the wicked Queen a chance."

"That should be easy enough," Anna reassures the old friend quickly. "The rules seem to be quite simple."

"Simple or not, they are very important, otherwise we all could be in danger!"

Otto shudders. It is quite funny, when he does that, his whole body makes a noise like rustling leaves in the autumn.

"Well, dear, just keep looking out for her before she can get a hold of you with that vicious veil of hers, that's the best. Keep practising looking for the signs of acute anger approaching! Practice, Anna, practice," Toady looks at Anna's eyes.

That very moment, Anna cannot help herself. She feels a familiar rush of heat, puts her legs slightly apart, and shouts: "I hate that word. Practice. Are you just like the teachers and Mummy? It does not help. I have tried and tried." She feels quite upset.

"Please Anna, quick, calm down! Do not get angry before it is too late! The Queen!!"

Both, Otto and Toady are urging her at the same time.

"Oh, so sorry," Anna says, as she realises she is endangering them all. "I don't mean it, really. I am not angry, just sad."

"I know, dear Anna. Still, a close call. I forgive you for using that word – 'hate'. We call it the 'h' word. It is not really used here. It belongs to the words of the others, the slaves of the wicked creature. One example of the stuff you have to watch out for. But you are new. A lot of learning. And practice, darling, I am afraid. It does help. But you have to practise things you know and understand. Then it works. You will even like it! Promise!"

She smiles at Anna, glad that she has managed to calm the girl down in time.

"I will get you on our program as soon as I can. You are a fast learner, I can tell."

"Anyhow," she says as she turns and walks to a different part in the hollow. "Come and help me a bit with my work. All that lichen in that corner needs to be turned over for drying. It is such a good harvest. We use the plant for a really nice winter vegetable, as well as filling for mattresses and so."

Anna and Otto both get stuck in to the task. Anna loves it. It is like working in a farmyard, something she's always fancied doing.

Suddenly, both Otto and Anna stop and lift their heads. They hear a strange noise combined with soft vibrations of the ground where they are standing. Anna is a little frightened. What is that? An earthquake? The noise is definitively coming from somewhere in the soil.

She looks over to her companion. To her great relief, he is giving her a 'thumbs up' and tells her smilingly: "Hey Anna, can you hear the mole? That is a good sign. He is taking someone back. Maybe the program is finished. Come on, let's go outside and have a look."

As they are walking out of the hollow, Anna watches something really strange. The earth in front of the old oak tree seems to move. A few meters away from them a huge hill appears.

Someone sneezes.

"Oh, excuse me, my dears. The soil is terribly dry today. Got right up into my nose." A fully-grown mole digs himself out of the top of the hill. He sneezes again, then takes off his glasses and squints down at Otto and Anna.

Anna has never seen a mole that close in real life. He looks very friendly and his fur appears extremely soft. The round spectacles on his nose make his tiny eyes look a bit larger.

He struggles to climb down and walks in a funny way closer towards them.

He stretches his right very large front paw out to Otto and Mrs Toad, who by now has come out as well to greet the new arrival.

Then he takes his glasses of, gives them a quick rub on his fur, before putting them back and coming up very close to Anna.

"And who have we got there? Are you the new candidate? Are my poor little eyes right in telling me this is a girl? Oh, how nice. We had so many boys in the last spell. A nice change. Oh dear, forgetting my manners. What is your name," he asks as he is stretches out his oversized paw again, this time for Anna to shake. She loves the softness of the skin, so much softer and dryer than people's hands.

Anna introduces herself.

Then he says: "My name is Rupert. Rupert the mole. In charge of the underground transport system. We call it the 'tube' for short. I've just taken the recent graduate to the exit tunnel. We had great fun. We were both giggling and joking. A lot better than when he joined the scheme."

He turns round to Mrs Toad. " I tell you, Mrs Boss, good choices. It is so nice to know there are so many successful gifted kids joining the Chosen. No couch potatoes, I tell you. No, they are lively and constantly looking out for more things to do. Great ideas."

Mrs Toad smiles at him and asks: "My friend Isolde Owl must be very pleased. She really did finish the program with him very quickly."

"Bright lad he was. He'll go a long way." Rupert looks very pleased. He only does some of the transport, but gets very attached to his customers.

Mrs Toad turns round and explains to Anna: "This is just right for you. Next time you come, Rupert can take you in his underground system to Isolde Owl's institute. It is at the other side of the park close to the river. It is safer to take the tube for that distance. Less chance of being trampled on by big people.

Isolde Owl designs and teaches the best programs known for children. She is just fabulous. Never known to fail any of her young friends."

Otto and Rupert are nodding in agreement. But Anna feels a bit nervous. Is it not quite dangerous to go into an underground tunnel? She has heard stories of children getting trapped and suffocating in tunnels they had dug for themselves.

She is just about to ask when Otto's Scottish voice comes in:

"Hey, cheer up, young lassie. Nothing to worry about. Isolde will be great for you and with regards to the tunnel, all folks get a wee bit worried the first time they're invited. But let me tell you. Rupert is the master of his craft and his tube is the best. Safe as houses, so they say. You'll have fun."

"Have provided safe underground service for a long time," Rupert says, making a funny little bow towards Anna. This nearly sends him falling over because his small back feet are barely able to carry his body.

Anna is still chuckling when she thinks back to his cute little gesture. He'd looked so serious and proud, before he had to use his digging paws for balance. But now it is seriously time for her to make her way back up, to go home. She can't risk any more trouble with her parents than she is already in. She excuses herself, bids farewell and is happy for Otto to take her back to the bottom of the toadstool. She manages to imagine the sun shining through her tear and enjoys it when the rainbow spirals her back up.

Later on, when her parents sit her down, she is amazed how much Mrs Toad's advice helps her talk to them. For the first time, she manages to explain how she feels.

"Oh, Mummy and Daddy," her voice is all shaky. "I know I have no excuse for being a horrible girl. I feel really bad about what I have done. But you know, it was a build up of what had happened. I was so confused in the morning. I got my clothes wrong. I don't know why. But then when I got my tables all muddled in the car and all. I don't know, I just felt really bad. I hate it when people laugh about my mistakes. And then it got to me when Amanda was showing off. I just got so angry. It was like I was blind, or so. I know it's no excuse… I promise. It'll never happen again. I feel so bad," she says, starting to cry a little.

Her parents are very surprised. Anna had never shown before how deeply bothered she was about her problems with learning her tables and other things. They had always just thought that maybe she hadn't tried hard enough.

"Anna, you are suddenly so more grown up. It's no excuse, but at least you admit that your behaviour was unacceptable. Of course, we still have to punish you, but…"

Mum and Dad look at each other before they tell her: "No TV, no pocket money, no computer games, no activities. It all starts from now on for at least four weeks. Then we'll sit together again and review it. See if you have learned a lesson. Every day you come home and sit down to do your homework, no argument.

Then you'll get a bit extra.

Again, no argument.

Mum will keep a score sheet.

Agreed?"

Anna lets her head hang down. Her parents can barely hear her little voice when she says: "Yes, Mummy and Daddy. I am really sorry. I promise I will not argue and I try to do my homework and everything you said. But what about my training, my running?"

She is terribly worried that she has ruined everything. Now that she has finally got a place with Isolde Owl.

Her parents hesitate for a moment and look at each other with that, 'Not so sure, what do you think, darling,' expression before her Mum says: "I think some physical activity is good for you. So. Yes, you can go for your run. But straight back, you know. No hanging around. I'll watch the time."

Anna can hardly suppress a grin. No TV, no money, no computer... so what! She'll still be able to go back to the Chosen! See her friends. Go on the program! She just has to keep an eye on the time. Pity she finds it so hard to read her wristwatch. She'll just have to guess.

In her bedroom, she tucks her herbs under her pillow, makes sure the leaf with the cream is safely put away for the next day and falls into a deep exhausted sleep in no time at all.

THE LIBRARY

Anna has to spend a lot of time in the library. Her work is set out by her teacher.

As usual, she finds it hard.

She has to write a story. It's supposed to be a fantasy story.

'Wow, if only anybody knew...' she thinks to herself. 'I could tell a good story.'

But firstly: she is not allowed. Remember the *Rules* !

Secondly: she can never write down what is in her head anyway.

Instead, she imagines brilliant pictures. Gargoyles, grotesque faces, flying down from the top of the facades of Oxford's colleges. Some of them are animals, but she has often wondered who the others might be.

Maybe she could hitch a ride on the back of a griffin? Flying through crowded streets, knocking off people's hats. What a laugh. They would not know what was happening. They would not want to admit they had seen a girl on the back of a griffin. Ha ha, they might think they had eaten some poison or were still drunk after a night out.

Maybe, even better, she could fly along the canal and look into the windows of the narrow boats.

They look so nice and she is sure that the people on them are fun. They wouldn't mind a griffin and a girl.

Then she would fly on into town and land on top of one of the highest towers. She now can almost see the busy life below her. Streets full of the tiniest people, rushing around, busy, shopping, catching busses, going to work. Some homeless person sitting on a blanket, usually with a dog. Begging. Mummy always tells her to look the other way.

"We give enough to their charities. Don't give them any money. It's only for drinks and drugs."

But she does wonder sometimes. In her favourite fairytales, you have to give them money or food. They are usually good people, just very poor. Sometimes, they're noble people, bewitched, waiting to be released from their ordeal.

"My goodness, Anna! Are you dreaming or are you working?" The harsh voice of the teacher supervising the kids in trouble in the library sharply interrupts her daydream.

"Sorry, Miss. Have to write a story and I'm trying to think of something."

"Obviously, you have not even started! What does that say?" She points to one rather untidily scribbled line on the top of her page. She translates her scribbles.

Anna sometimes writes very small and untidily. She knows that some teachers can't read it and she can hide her bad spellings.

"An aedvnshastoy"

"It says: An adventure story."
"Hey, at least you can read your own stuff. Come on, let me help you. Let me correct those spellings."

Anna is grateful. She knows that after a while, even she is not able to decipher her writing. And correcting after copying takes her ages too!

A deep sigh comes from her. The teacher seems quite nice for a change, she is trying to help her further.

"Come on, let's have a go together. You start writing and I'll sit beside you. Then I can help your spellings straight away."

This is very nice of her, but in the end it does not really work. She writes two sentences. Beautiful, but not a story:

'One day I walked through Oxford. I saw some gargoyles.'

She spends a huge amount of time writing *gargoyles* in different versions, even after the teacher has spelled it out for her. She just gets it wrong again and again.

"Excuse me please, Miss. My nose is running." She pretends to need a handkerchief.

In reality, she has just felt her anger build up; anger about stupid spellings and not being able to write her story the way she wants to. But for the first time in her life, she recognises that what she has felt are a few red hot tentacles of anger, signs of the Queen of fury touching her cheeks!

She must not allow her to be able to get a hold on her. Instead of her hanky, she quickly takes out the tiny leaf from her pocket and very carefully applies some of the cream to her earlobes.

'Hope it works,' she thinks. She can feel her heart beating fast and hard, racing in a built up to an angry fit.

She hears a strange noise, almost like water being poured over a hot surface. Then she can just make out the edges of a red veil being pulled away from her and disappearing fast behind some library books.

'It worked!' She has escaped! Not only has she managed to recognise the first signs of anger, but also nearly saw the Queen herself!

She knows now, she is learning to be one of the Chosen.

The kind teacher praises her pathetic little work: "Well done, Anna! You now have a nice little start to your nice little story. Next time you come, I will sit down straight away with you.

You'll soon see what a nice little story the two of us can write down together."

Anna politely thanks her. But deep down she thinks: "Nice little story, nice little... pooh. She should see the real thing."

Later, after school, the teachers all have a class council. The nice teacher is the only one who has anything positive to say about Anna.

"She did try really hard. You should have seen her. Her face was really red with the effort in the end. I think she needs some more help and support," she tells her colleagues.

They only look at each other. The teacher is well known amongst the staff for her 'softly, softly' approach.

They snigger.

THROUGH THE TUNNELS

The day passes with no further occurrences. After doing her homework as best as she can, Anna gets her running gear out.

Her sister is sitting in her own room with the door open.

No sooner does she spot Anna, she shouts: "You are not allowed to go to activities. Mum 'n Dad said. I have to keep an eye on you before mummy gets in. So you better stay or else – I'll tell!"

Anna is clenching her teeth. Then she replies: "I am going for running training. I am allowed! So shut up, or else...'

'Oh no, careful, not the Queen again,' she says to herself, taking a deep breath. The leaf with the anti-anger cream is in the other trousers. Will there be enough time?

She quickly runs back to her room and retrieves the precious leaf. But before she can even apply the cream, Anna realises that she has managed to calm herself down. There is no veil anywhere near her.

"I am really learning, practising and getting better at it," she thinks happily as she skips towards the park.

She manages to squeeze out one or two tears, and in no time at all finds herself back in the land of the Chosen.

No sooner has she arrived, Anna spots Oskar the ant. He appears to have been waiting for her.

"Hi Anna. Great. You are here. I am supposed to take you for a ride to the entrance of the molehill. Rupert will take you from there through the underground system. Mrs Owl is ready for you. You'll love the program. They all do."

Despite all of the reassurances, Anna has a few butterflies in her tummy.

But before she can think too much, Oskar lowers his hind legs to let her climb onto his back.

"I am riding an ant!" She is thrilled. It is not easy to sit on Oskar as his skin is very hard and slippery. But she manages.

"If Otto can do this, I can," she thinks to herself whilst holding on strongly to the front part of the ant's body.

On the way, Oskar tells her about the way that moles and ants work together: "We are the inter-park transport system. But we also run a different kind of business: 'Communication'! I can sense a lot of information with my antennae and pass it on to the moles by stamping my feet. Moles have superb hearing. They decode our messages and quickly pass them on."

"So cool," Anna replies. "You don't need mobile phones here. Ha, that's funny. In Germany, they call them 'handy'. You could call yours 'footsy'," she giggles.

Anna slides down off his back when they arrive at the molehill.

Rupert greets her with a welcoming smile and a wave with one of his enormous hands.

"Come on then. I'll go down into the tunnel first, then you just hold onto my back. I'll guide you."

It is so dark in the tunnel. 'This is how blind people must feel,' she thinks as she follows the mole. He is digging a tube with surprising speed, pushing his way forward. Anna can smell the slight damp earthy smell of the surrounding soil. She is surprised that the tunnel is firm and smooth. She had thought it would be crumbly and sticky.

She keeps a firm hold of Rupert's soft fur as she follows him steadily through the narrow tunnels. Occasionally, she finds they are meeting adjoining tubes with other moles, always exchanging polite greetings as they pass each other. She cannot see them but her sense of hearing appears to be very sharp and alert.

After what seemed ages, they suddenly pop up into the brightness of daylight and find themselves on the top of yet another molehill.

Right in front of them rises the gigantic stem of a very old willow tree.

"Must be close to the river," Anna realises.

On the bottom of the gnarly old tree, she spots a sign. She has to squint because of the bright light. She tries to read what it says:

PRIVATE INSTITUTE

ISOLDE OWL

TOP HOLE

3RD BRANCH

The mole, who is used to children struggling with the changes in light, reads it out to her. "Means we are here," he adds.

"How can I possibly get to the top hole?" Anna asks anxiously. The stem is enormous.

She can just make out the top hole by bending her head right back.

There are a few others on the way up, on all sides of the stem.

But there is only one top one at the third branch.

"Follow me," Rupert the mole says.

He leads her through a narrow crack in the back of the stem. She hadn't noticed that entrance at all before. How clever! It is rather dimly lit inside the stem, but moles do not need light. So he safely leads her to the bottom of some wooden ladders.

"Well, have to leave you here. My little legs will never make it up the steps. I'll collect you here later, Anna, after your first session. Take care." He waddles away.

Anna is very careful as she begins to climb up the ladder. There are a few platforms. Each one has a hole where there must have been branches in the tree's youth. Now they are useful windows that let in some light.

Each platform seems to form a different kind of room.

The bottom one resembles a classic type of schoolroom, just with very few desks.

The next one is a fun and games room. After another climb up, Anna arrives in a room full of little hammocks. When she stops to catch her breath back she sees that they are not ordinary hammocks. They are made of densely woven spider webs, each containing blankets and pillows of the finest silky cocoon material.

"How strange and cute," Anna thinks.

Finally, she arrives at the top floor.

A deep voice, almost hooting, greets her:

"Welcome Anna. I have been waiting for you. My name is Isolde Owl. Most of my customers call me Isy or Owly. Whatever you prefer. Come and take a seat. Quite a climb, eh? I never have to do it. Just fly in and out of the holes," she smiles. "But exercise is good for young ones. If I have older customers, which is very rarely, or some that have difficulties walking, I call an air taxi, usually provided by the bats." Anna has only seen owls in the wildlife park before. She has visited a few times, but she was more interested in the penguins waddling about and some of the other animals. Now she looks at the big bird standing right in front of her. Owly has very big eyes, which have a friendly brown colour. Her wing feathers make no sound in the air as she talks and points to things like we do with our hands. Even though she has a big curved beak, she manages to smile at the girl. "Come on then, Isy doesn't bite. But I am dying for a nice cuppa."

There is a very comfortable sofa on one of the walls, flanked by two cosy chairs. Anna sits down on one of them.

To her surprise, a small door that she had not even noticed before opens and a strange insect walks in, carrying a tea tray.

"My assistant, Woody Woodborer," Isy says, introducing the newcomer. "He makes an excellent bark tea and his resin biscuits, wow, I tell you, they are divine!" She clicks her tongue. "Please, do tuck in!"

Anna feels quite hungry and thirsty. As she takes a little bite of her biscuit, she cannot believe what's happening. Her whole mouth and nose seems to be filled with an unbelievably strong herbal scent.

"This is delicious!" she exclaims.

She has never in her life tasted such a beautiful flavour before.

Woody smiles, very pleased with her response.

"They are lovely, aren't they? Only the finest resin from young trees will do."

Anna leaves one biscuit on the plate. Politeness. She does not want to appear greedy. Then she drinks a sip of her tea. Again, what beautiful flavours, they're almost magical!

Isy smiles at her: "Good, no?"

"Fantastic," Anna reaffirms.

THE PROGRAM

Isy tells Anna to climb down into the schoolroom whilst she flies out of one hole, and in no time at all, into the next. She is standing by the front of the room, next to a desk, ready and waiting, before Anna has made it down the ladders.

It feels very strange to her to be the only pupil in the classroom. She glances around for clues to see if there is anyone else joining.

The old owl has seen her searching looks, and as if magically reading her mind, tells her: "Every child is different, Anna. We like to give you a chance to see what type of learning works best for you. Your program will be designed and performed just for you. That is why we are so different.

Now, my lovely, what do you think is the most important thing for you to start on? What would you really like to improve the most?"

Anna does not hesitate and immediately exclaims: "I am total and utter rubbish at spelling; well, writing and reading. I cannot learn it. I am really stupid, you know. I don't think anyone can help me with that really. So many have tried." She looks quite upset.

"The art of words it will be then," the owl replies without hesitation.

"The art of words?" Anna asks, feeling bewildered.

"Yes dear, the art of words. Words are indeed pieces of art. They all look different, they have meanings, and they even have different music.

And like pictures, you can look at them and decide that you either like them or not. You might understand them; they can make you feel like something... Phoo. I could carry on about this, but I think it is high time to get started. After that, you will need no further explanations."

With that she flaps her wings together like clapping hands, and what before had just looked like a normal whiteboard, turns out to be a live stage with lots of little doors in it, similar to an advent calendar.

One of the doors opens and a strange kind of worm or caterpillar wiggles out of it. It moves right across the board. In its front legs it carries the letter 'A', both capital and small. It gives off a bizarre noise, like music or chanting, as it is crosses the board sounding out the letter. The noise sounds like it comes from well inside Anna's head. It's not unpleasant, but a bit like the noise a balloon makes when it's popped too close to your ear.

"What is that?" Anna shouts out in surprise at the strange sensation she feels.

"That, Anna, is your first ear worm. Isn't it great? Listen to it! You'll remember the sound and the name of the little worm."

Anna thinks it is hilarious. There is tickling in both of her ears, as if the worm has actually made its way right through her head, in one ear and out through the other. First left, then right, at the same way as it is wiggling across the board.

"Now, Anna, close your eyes!" the owl commands.

"What can you see and hear?"

Like in a photo slideshow on the computer, the letter 'A' appears in her imaginary eye, and at the same time, she can hear the sound of the earworm deep inside her head.

"This is magic! How do you do that?" she shouts excitedly.

"It is really easy. It is the magic of our earworms. They introduce themselves with the sound they make. Most of them only make one sound. But there are special ones, like this one. They make more then one. Easy peasy, japaneasy! Hoot, hoot, hoot," she laughs.

"Can I have more?" Anna asks eagerly.

She spends a good while with the earworms. One after the other they appear and make their funny little wiggle and music as they move across the board, and every time she gets that weird but nice sensation in her ears.

She is loving it. They all give a slightly different performance. After every one of them, Anna is asked to close her eyes and listen to her own head echoing the sound of the letter she 'sees'.

"This is magic, Isy. You magicked all the letters into my head!"

"Not me, my dear. It is the earworm's performance," the owl replies modestly.

In no time at all the cute little worms have passed all the letters into Anna's head.

It did not feel like any learning, rather like watching a live performance or a very entertaining film.

"More, more!" she demands when they have at last reached the letter 'z'.

"No, Anna. That would not be good," Isy Owl replies. "You'll end up with all sorts of earworms in a wiggly tangle. Then nothing would be gained. You are best to return home now. Have a good night's sleep. Dream about the worms, words and pieces of art. I am a night owl. I will go for a really good flight out. Nightlife around here is really great at the moment for us owls," she laughs with a very loud hoot, obviously looking forward to her flight. Then, as if from nowhere, Woody appears.

"Please take Anna back down for her transport. We are done for the day. Thanks, Woody." She stretches her wings and her legs, which make a slight clicking sound, as she is not the youngest.

But Anna pleads with her: "Please, Isy. Before I go, can I ask you some questions I have been so intrigued about since I arrived here?"

The owl looks at the girl with her big eyes, and with this wink, she answers in a slow, long drawn out way: "Yes, what questions would those be?"

"I have been passing through this other room that's full of comfortable looking hammocks. So inviting! Please, can I stay there?"

The owl is shaking her head; the way only owls can, right round and back again.

"No, Anna, no. That does not suit you, Anna. You have some loving parents. They would miss you and get very upset. These hammocks are for little orphans or children that are not missed by anybody, because they are not loved. These children need the cushions spun with loving care by caterpillars, the way they make their own cocoons. This helps their sleep when the big change is coming for them, when they turn into butterflies or moths. Before these poor children grow up, they need doses of this good sleep, with love woven in for them. It gives them a chance of a brighter future and makes them learn to love others.

You do not need that, Anna. You can do that already."

She winks her slow shutter wink again: "Now, off you go home and, Anna, don't forget to dream!"

She nods a farewell and flies out of the tree hole.

Woody hops down the ladder with Anna to the waiting Rupert at the molehill.

In no time at all, he whizzes her back through the tunnel system, back to the toadstool and the moss cushion.

She follows her usual routine for returning via the rainbow spiral.

"Very strange, but Anna appears so much happier these days," her father comments to his wife just after he has tucked both girls into their beds that night. He always stays for a little while with each of them. He is used to Louisa always happily chatting to him, telling him her newest success stories. Anna, meanwhile, usually cries and moans about something that has happened, at least during term time, or complains about some tummy aches and pains she gets when she's had another bad day. But tonight she happily chirped about some things she appeared to be interested in, about the cycle of life of butterflies and owls, for example.

"Anna likes nature. Maybe no TV does her a lot of good," Dad says with a hopeful smile on his face.

BACK IN CLASS

After a really refreshing night's sleep, where her dreams were filled with pictures of rainbows, dancing worms and singing letters, Anna manages to get ready for school without too many muddles and in reasonable time.

"It must be the fish oil kicking in," her mum thinks, looking at her younger daughter. "Her eyes are so much brighter, even her skin looks healthier. I never used to believe in all these natural remedies before but – well they used to give it to us when we were little, maybe it does work. After all, it was recommended by Professor Rock."

She hasn't got a clue about wise owls, gentle toads, mole tunnels or earworms!

"Just as well," Anna thinks to herself. Otherwise, she would start overdramatising: dangerous tunnels, poisonous toadstools, weird-looking Scottish strangers in the park, and so on."

In class, they have to read some worksheets for science. Usually, she cheats, listening carefully to what all the others say, trying to get the gist. But today, something new happens. As she is looking at the words on her sheet, she suddenly hears the earworms singing out the sounds of the letters.

Slowly, very slowly, she finds she can make out the words, much better then she ever did before.

"Wow, word art. Art of words. Surely less scary than ordinary reading." Anna is very pleased about her progress. She can barely wait for the next part of her program.

Nobody else in class has noticed any change in her reading. She has always been exceptionally clever at hiding her shortfall.

Some time later in the library, she meets up with Philip, who is in trouble again after hiding the Maths teacher's calculator. This did not amuse the poor man, who now has to work out the answers himself.

Philip got caught when he secretly used the electronic gadget to do his own work.

"Pooh, deep trouble. They even accuse me of stealing! Not fair. 'Never steal', I said. 'And what do you think, taking your teacher's calculator amounts to, young man?' they said. They only believe what they want to or they think they see. Was only a joke. To see the poor bloke struggle and sweat. And then. Might as well use it, had it under my desk. Would have been such a waste of a perfectly good calculator, wouldn't it, Anna?"

He looks at her to reassure himself before he continues in a much sadder whisper: "I'll get my hide seen to by my old man tonight. He is very good at that. Always does it in places where nobody can see the marks afterwards. As if I would tell anyway! Nobody'll believe me, him being that doctor for kids. Haha. So funny. Don't know how he manages to be nice to them. Just can't stand me, suppose, and my mum that is. She gets his temper too."

"Shh! You two. You are supposed to work. Not to waste each other's time with chitchats," Mrs James' voice sharply interrupts them.

Philip rolls his eyes and picks up his workbook. Very, very gently he starts to tear out the page on which his work is set out. He tries not to make any noise whilst doing this. Anna, however, is a very alert girl. She notices and starts a silent giggle. She can't believe what she is observing.

'What on earth is the boy doing?' He is now putting the torn out page in his mouth. 'This is hilarious!' she thinks when he is actually chewing on the paper and next, swallowing it.

'Why does he do that?'

Next thing: he does it again with another page. And Again!

Suddenly, Mrs James, who had been totally engrossed in some of her own work, jumps up, grabs his book and shouts: "You silly boy, what are you doing? You can't eat your Maths book!"

"Excuse me Miss, don't want to be disrespectful, but Miss, sorry, I can."

"Philip, this is not funny. This is the strangest behaviour I have ever seen." Anna stops laughing. "This is serious!" she adds with a sideway glance at the girl.

"Of course, I will report this to your form teacher, the head, as well as your parents. And on your behaviour sheet, I can't even put a sad face. This is so bizarre. I'll have to have a chat with the colleagues... Been in teaching such a long time, never..."

Anna hears her mumbling, obviously deeply shocked. "...Retirement... not soon enough..."

Anna looks at Philip. 'Wow he must be so brave. She would never dare to do anything like that,' she thinks.

He grins at her. But when she looks carefully, she can detect some sadness deep down in his big brown eyes.

"Is this just a show?' she wonders.

She slides him a secret note:

"Laets meat afta scuol."

It will be difficult to meet him because she is collected by car, as usual.

Maybe she could pretend to have an extra sports lesson, in preparation for the big race.

In the end, she does make up a good enough excuse for the mum who is on collecting that day.

She also claims that Philip's mum will take her home, so no worries.

'Yeah, one hour of complete freedom!' she laughs to herself. Pity she can't take Philip to the park to introduce him to her little friends. But rules are rules!

Philip walks slowly home with her and tells her about his anger at everyone, and his parents especially. Well, his mum is sort of OK, he explains.

"Except she is too weak to stand up to him. When Dad gets angry with me – about a hundred times a week – she just cries and asks me why I am such a bad boy. Don't know, really, don't wanna be. Just comes to me by accident. Enjoy the fun when others are laughing, like you did when I ate my book. By the way, don't try it. Tastes really ghastly. Disgusting! Yuck!" He smiles at her.

"My little sister is such a good girl. Daddy really loves her. He says, he'll really love me too, except I am so bad. Makes it difficult for him.

I think one day I'll run away. They'll be better off without me." There is a tear glistening in the corner of both his eyes.

There is a hard lump in Anna's throat. "You can't do that! It's far too dangerous. There are bad people waiting to take children away. Please don't do it!" She is pleading with him. Anna thinks that she urgently needs to talk to her little friends, especially Mrs Toad. Surely they would understand that Philip needs them?

She listens with horror to Philip's story.

"Anna, it's quite weird, but you know, deep down I think I still love him. And he always says he loves me, but then I just can't help it. I don't want to be bad. Just get carried away. I think it's a joke. Nobody else does. Then I just... it just comes out of nowhere, you know. I just get a hundert percent angry! Fuse blown. That's it."

Anna can see some water in the corner of his eyes. With an irritable, "Jeez. Now I'm bubbling. Great. What a hero I am," he wipes his nose with the back of his hand. "Maybe him and I, we are just the same. Mind you, when he gets angry, wow. Can't really tell you, but hey, bruises in the right places! Nobody can see them. Anyway, who would care? They all just think it's from one of my fights.

"...Then Dad usually ends up crying. Me too. But it is always me who makes him cry. It's me, I make him do bad things to me. So wicked. So bad."

Anna feels a lump in her throat. She can't believe what he is telling her. She must find help for him.

"Dad says he is normally such a good man. Always helping other children. Puh, so what? That's no good to me. I don't know where I get it from. Not from Mum, that's for sure. I get very angry. Could hit him too. Want to, but don't. He's my dad."

He gives a little grin. "But, I tell you, when other kids upset me, I tell them in no uncertain way! I have my own personal style," he sniggers.

Anna shudders. A cold wave seems to travel down her back. She would love to tell him about the Queen of Fury. But – it's not allowed! She really must have a word...

EARWORMS

Anna enjoys the program with Isy Owl and her earworms very much.

She has been back a few times. She is very used to travelling underground with Rupert or one of the other moles, if he is not available.

The little earworms are now dancing in groups together. Sometimes, as many as four in one formation, making one kind of sound together, showing the letters that go with it. She is amazed.

She only needs to see the little groups together, just like a picture in her head, and she automatically hears the sound they make.

Her reading is now really speeding up. She even starts to enjoy spotting all the little earworms together on a page in school. It is all coming together.

Isy is asking her in one of her sessions if she would like to create some word art herself.

"I love making art," she eagerly replies.

Instead of pens and paper, she is being given sheets made of white birch bark. They have a lovely scent! Then she gets a paintbrush which looks rather strange. A bit like a child's magic wand.

"Take the sounds out of your head, just as they are, with your word art pen and watch what happens," her owl teacher instructs her.

Anna is a bit puzzled, but she does as she is told and is very surprised when she sees what the magic that the brush produces on the bark sheet.

Lots of groups of letters are forming and dancing at the same time as they appear to be singing in her head. There are the pictures of the earworms underneath each group, holding on to each other in a chain, like little boat shapes.

Now, as she looks again at the beautiful creation on her bark, she suddenly realises that she has written lots of words. She is so excited. She cannot stop herself from creating more and more words. This is so easy and so much fun. She is laughing out aloud.

The earworms are smiling back at her. Why has she never met them before? This is crazy. She could write any story using them!

One of the little worms in a rather large formation winks at her. They seem to enjoy her word art as well.

"Did I write all of that?" she cries in astonishment.

"Well Anna, I knew you would be gifted the minute I saw you. Not many children can make the earworms dance so quickly!" she smiles encouragingly. "When you are back at your own school, all you have to do is to let the earworms dance in your head when you want to write. You'll soon see that they follow you there and help you to write all the sounds that you need. Let them sing and dance in their little groups!"

"More, more. I want to learn more!" She is very keen indeed.

But again, as before, the wise bird stops her from overcharging her head: "Anna, it is fantastic how you've learned to handle the worms so quickly, but now it is time for you to return. We don't want knots in their chains. You now need to go back, and I am afraid to say, you need to practise

>practise

>practise

handling them."

There are those most hated words again! But to her astonishment, she no longer feels bad about them – the opposite, really. She can hardly wait to see if the worms dance for her when she is using ordinary paper and pen, instead of the magic brush and the bark.

She feels like floating back through the tube. She is very thrilled but remembers that she has a mission. She asks Otto to take her briefly to Mrs Toad. Philip has had a few very bad days and she has to help him. Anna is now getting really worried about his threat of running away.

"You see, Mrs Owl, I think he has issues with the Queen of Fury. He and his Dad just get so angry, they can't stop. His Dad can be really bad to him. Do grown-ups get trapped in the angry veil as well?"

Mrs Owl takes a moment before she answers: "Anger is what she lives off. She does not mind where it comes from. We can usually help children to learn to recognise the Queen approaching. It is much more difficult with adults. They are so used to live the way they live. They can't change easily. "

"But we must find a way to help Philip. I think he is actually a nice boy underneath it all."

She explains to Mrs Owl how hard it has been for her not to tell him about the evil Queen of Fury. She talks about all his worries and his sorrows. All the trouble he is getting himself into.

Mrs Toad is very moved. She snivels a bit and takes her glasses off as she quickly wipes her eyes.

"Well. I must say, I have heard about this boy before. I would love to help, but there is danger. He is so unable to control his anger. Obviously, the Queen of Fury has got a strong hold on him." She sighs deeply.

"He could endanger all of us. The wicked creature is waiting to invade our land. She has tried before. Last time, it was a little girl who brought her in. She did not mean to, but we nearly lost it. I do not want to frighten you with the story, but I tell you that it was very close, very close indeed." Anna feels a cold shiver go down her spine.

"We barely managed to escape a catastrophe. Though we did, as you can tell. We don't harbour any anger in our community."

But Anna still pleads: "If I talk to Philip and explain the whole problem to him, and warn him to be careful? Please, Toady, he is so desperately unhappy. He needs us!"

"I know your motives are very noble and that you are trustworthy. But, I don't know. I just have a bad feeling."

Anna looks very upset.

Toady's kind eyes don't miss it. She says: "Maybe, with a friend like you, maybe he is ready for us? But on a trial base only. Please do not tell him how to get here. Just take him along with you. Just for this one occasion, I allow you to share your tear with him.

Anna is very relieved.

"I am sure he can shed loads of tears himself. I know he comes across as one of these tough boys, but I am certain I saw some tears glistening in his eyes the other day," Anna says, surprised that she should share her tears.

"Oh, Anna. I am sure he has, but they might be the wrong type of tears. That could be dangerous. You know there are several different varieties of tears; those of joy, desperation or anger. The ones we need to ride the spiral are the ones of sorrow."

"Desperation, anger, sorrow, what is the difference?" Anna asks. "Surely a tear is a tear?"

"Oh no, Anna. There is a big difference. We can't allow angry tears to be used! They are highly dangerous. They are the disguises of the Queen of Fury. We only allow children with real sad tears to come. So, please don't tell him to use his own tears. He might be sad, but I have a feeling his tears are highly contaminated by anger! In his circumstances, I think we are better off sharing a tear." She looks very serious and a bit worried. Then, in deep thought, she adds: "Maybe he is a more suitable candidate for bat transport."

"Bat transport? " Anna exclaims with surprise.

"For the sleepovers at Isy's, that is. You know, for the sad unloved children. Remember the hammocks? Quietly, at night, after lights out, the bats come and fly in through some small openings. They pick up the children in the dark. Bats don't need light. They find their way by using echo sound. It's so high pitched, grown-ups can't hear them. But the children do. They jump on their backs and are flown straight to Mrs Owl's. They get the best night's sleep anyone can have on the little pillows spun from the softest silk. In their dreams, they learn the art of love. The blankets are made of butterfly wings, soft and dusted with colourful powder, brightening up the grey of their life.

Before dawn, the children are back in their own beds. Nobody has noticed their flight on the bat. But the children are very much happier afterwards."

"I don't know if you could fly Philip out so easily. He leaves his door open, he's told me, because he sometimes has such bad nightmares, he screams. Then his mum comes."

"Ah, that is good to hear. Obviously his mum does love him. Maybe there is hope we can just help him here then. Maybe he fights the Queen off in his sleep. Anna, just promise to be careful. Make sure that he is not in an angry mood. Can I trust you to judge that? And please don't let him know what you are doing to get to us." Mrs Owl still looks unconvinced.

"I promise, Mrs Owl! I will be ever so careful. I'll talk to him beforehand and see what mood he is in. I won't bring him if he is angry. Only if he is sad."

Mrs Owl and her friends have heard about Philip. They know that he is one of the Queen's favourites. The tiny mosquitoes have told her. Sometimes, they sample tiny drops of blood from children when they sleep. They can taste it when children need to come here, to us. Only a small bump on the skin afterwards, that's slightly itchy, tells the child of the mosquito's visit.

Mrs Toad looks at Anna's eyes as she bids her goodbye. "Be very, very careful," she says with some dark foreboding.

HELPING PHILIP

At school, Anna is still sitting next to Emma. On the outside, nothing has changed. They have been friends for a long time. Emma has never minded that Anna looks at her work after she has finished. She used to feel sorry for her and so helped her to spot the odd mistake. Their friendship had more important matters to be busy with. Anna had the best ideas when it came to making up new games. She also always had a way of involving other kids, and she had helped Em to master a simple spin on the crossbar. Emma is tidy in her work, Anna messy. In a way, they had always needed each other.

Anna is just finishing her writing, copying something of the whiteboard and filling in the blanks. Easy. "That is for kids that are normal," she thinks with envy her eyes, glancing casually over to Emma's neat work.

But instead of her friend pushing it over to her discretely, like usual, her left elbow goes 'bang', right over her page. "Surely, she seems to be hiding her work, it can't be true?" she thinks.

Anna's throat seems to have a big lump in it. Sad. "Em is so nice!"

Has this anything to do with Amanda?

Maybe it's because they can't be together at playtime?

Maybe Em did not have anyone else?
Maybe...

"Surely, when my detention is over, it'll be like normal again. Yes, sure. I'll show her a new trick on the crossbar. One leg only, backwards or so."

Anna secretly looks around at the other children in class. She catches Eliza's eyes. Is it her imagination or does she look quite strangely at her, with a kind of knowing expression. As if she wants to tell her something.

Weird! Anna has never bothered about Eliza before. She was just there. She's different. They had been told she needed special stuff. Lucky her. They allowed her to use a laptop because of her hands. Spell check and all, not fair!

Funny, suddenly Anna thinks of her. She had always been rubbish at Maths, just like her. Lower set. But hey, she had caught up with most of the others. How was that possible? "Must have cheated," Anna thinks. But had she? If so, how?

She looks at her again. Definitely, there is something. Eliza is mouthing something. Does it look like 'owl'? "Must be my imagination." Before she has a chance to mouth anything back, she gets a telling off from the teacher.

"Anna, for goodness sake. Stop ogling other people's stuff. Look at your own book. If you have a question, come to me. Leave the others."

"I'm only..."

"Quiet now."

No chance to find anything out at playtime. The library, naturally.

Today, it is that nicer teacher again. Better than Miss James.

Things are looking up, Anna thinks, as she remembers that her mum asked in the morning whether she would have that extra PE again.

"Yes," she thinks. "Going to meet up with Philip! Let's share a tear!"

He is in detention again as well, so she slips him a note in the library:

Meet me afta scool.

The earworms are great. They really help.

He nods his head slightly in answer to her secret note, so as not to be caught by the teacher, who is now sitting directly beside Anna and looking at the task she has been set.

"Let's see. Oh, lovely. Story writing again. Oh great, Anna. 'My favourite day'. Sure, you have a lot to write, eh, Anna? A nice little visit to your grandparents? Or playing in the swing park on a nice sunny day?"

She is trying to help.

Anna would have really liked to write about rainbow spirals, earworms dancing and ants drumming messages with their feet for moles to decode. But, of course, that would not be wise. Well, grandma and granddad will do. Swing park? Better not, too close to her adventures.

The kind teacher helps Anna with her spelling. She is surprised that Anna has written quite a bit and the spelling is not too bad.

"Oh, Anna, what a clever girl you are! This is so much better. I am sure you are my fastest little learner. I am so pleased for you. I knew it. All you need is a teacher who understands your problems."

Anna can't tell her about the earworms and owls. She smiles at her thinking: "At least she is trying. She is nice. I'll let her think it was her."

After school, Anna meets up with Philip.

"Hey Ann, don't know how you can stand that teacher at lunchtime. She would drive me nuts. Slime, slime." He looks into her eyes: "Never trust any of them! They just pretend. 'Oh, darling, you are soo good, you are amazing… Of course, it is me who is so amazing,' all that rubbish. Can't stand it."

Before he can carry on Anna interrupts him: "Calm down, man. I want to tell you something important. First, you have to swear not to tell anyone. It's a secret! Can I trust you?"

"Cross my heart," Philip reassures her.

She then tells him about Otto, Mrs Toad and the others, as well as about the Chosen and the secret land. She also tells him that they are really clever and help kids in need. And about anger and the enemy, the Queen, her veil and how she lives off the blind rage others get in.

He laughs at that. "Yeah, she must be getting quite fat on me, ha-ha." He does not really know if he should believe any of it. It just sounds too much like a story. But a good one. The red veil, that actually sounds familiar. He decides to test her.

"Come on, I want to go there. See them. How do we get there?"

"Not allowed to tell you. But if you trust me, I can take you. Just for a short trial period. I have got special permission. But you must stick to what I tell you. Promise? It could be dangerous otherwise."

Again Anna is warning him about the wicked Queen. She shows him the leaf with the cream and explains the purpose. As she takes the leaf out of her pocket, she realises in horror that it has almost dried out, as she has not needed it for a while. Maybe she is learning the signs?

It is a lovely afternoon, and when they arrive in the park it is quite lively – full of young people playing sports, kids on scooters, joggers, toddlers feeding ducks and some old people walking slowly. They giggle when they spot a boy and a girl kissing on one of the benches.

Philip can't believe there is another world here, other than what you see. But Anna is determined.

She leads him to the moss cushion and the toadstool.

"Please, do as I tell you, Phil. It is so important! Please?"

"OK, Anna, what do you think I am? I don't break a promise I've given to someone I like."

She blushes a bit. He likes her, he said so.

To be able to get to the land of the Chosen, she has to cry a tear of sorrow, which is quite difficult this time. But she thinks back to Emma and her nasty behaviour in class and the tears roll.

Philip is surprised by her mood, but has not much time to think about it as she is already rubbing his forehead as well as her own.

"Wheee, that is amazing," he shouts as they spiral down.

"Oh, wow, look at that mushroom thingy! It's a house! Hey, normally I kick the things over. Stupid things. But just as well I didn't!"

He looks around gobsmacked. He just can't believe what he is seeing.

"Was it the tear that got us here? Anna, tell me. You see I have plenty of those. Just have to think of everyone. My Dad. School. I get so upset and angry. See them, the tears?"

Anna shouts: "Stop, Stop. It's dangerous! I told you."

Philip looks very angry. "Nothing to do with you, Anna. Just can't help it. They just make me so upset. Want to hit them!"

Otto must have heard Anna's screams as he comes running out of his little cottage as fast as his knobbly legs can carry him.

"The cream. The cream! We need some of the emergency anti-anger cream!" Anna is so beside herself with fear, as she feels an incredible heat surrounding them.

She tries to dab some from her old leaf on her friend's ear. But it is too dry! It just crumbles under her fingers.

Otto has run back inside to grab a jar of cream and returns at an incredible speed, considering how short his legs are for such a heavy body.

Too late!

Philip is already covered in a huge red veil that has appeared from nowhere. The heat is unbearable. The sky is filled with a reddish fog, blanking out the sun that had shone so brightly at the innocent scene only a minute ago.

The air is filled with a strange buzzing sound, above which Anna and Otto can hear a very wicked laughter.

To her horror, Anna looks straight into the eyes of the evil Queen of Fury: "That'll teach you all a lesson! Hahaha. You cannot keep me out! Ha-ha-ha. The almighty Queen of Fury. Just found myself a nice easy slave from amongst you lot. Ha-ha. You think you won the battle. You thought you banned me. Ha-ha-ha-ha. You will see. I will get you all in the end! Hahahahaaar."

Her distorted terrible laugh is accompanied by a great orchestra of thousands of wasps that appear from all sides and pick up the edges of the Queen's veil. The terrified girl watches as her friend is wrapped into the net like a fly caught by a spider. Next, the whole thing is picked up and lifted into the air. The Queen of Fury picks some thin reins and lets out another cascade of shrill laughter as she leads the wasps on a flight away to an unknown destination. Philip's cries for help fade away as the kidnappers disappear behind the high grass on their flight.

In just one or two minutes, the whole spectacle is over.

For a moment they still hear the wasps humming and the evil Queen's voice seems to be singing something about a new slave.

Then there is nothing but their own fast breathing.

Anna throws her hands over her face and cries out: "What have I done? What have I done?"

Otto grabs her hands and shakes her shouting: "Don't just stand there! This is serious! We have to alert everyone! Our land is in danger!"

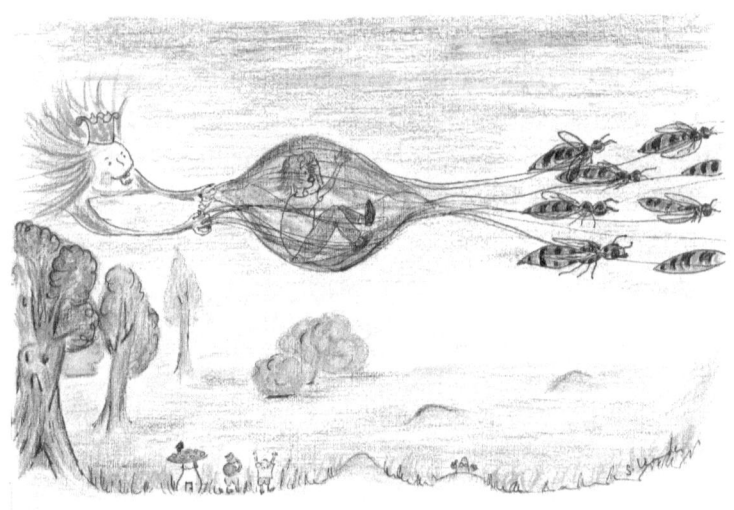

The first person they have to tell is Mrs Toad. She sinks back in horror onto one of her stools, throwing her arms up into the air: "I knew it, I knew it. I wish I had listened to my inner voice. Not again. Don't let it happen again. She'll come and take many of us." Her voice is very different to her normal one. There's no friendly croak this time, more of a moan.

"I am so sorry. So sorry. I didn't mean to. I tried to get him to calm again. But the cream had dried and he was so quick. So sorry," Anna's voice breaks away with her crying.

But Mrs Toad does not pay any attention to her. Her face is no longer a lovely soft shade of green, but a very deep olive colour instead.

"Well, my friends," she says as she stands up and pulls her dress down. "We need to react quickly.

We must declare a state of emergency. Otto, it's best if you tell Oscar to start all the ants on the foot drums. They need to spread the news and tell everyone to gather for an assembly. We have to make a plan of action, urgently! We must protect our land."

Anna's voice is barely loud enough to be heard when she asks: "What about Philip? Will he be her slave forever?"

"We'll try our best to help him, to free him from the wicked creature."

Toady looks sad and worried, but she does not show any anger about what has happened because Anna brought the boy down the spiral.

PHILIP

Philip has only flown on planes before. It is a weird sensation to be wrapped in a veil and carried through the air by the wasps.

Under better circumstances, he might have enjoyed the adventure. But now he is just frozen by fear and horror.

He realises that Anna's story about the Queen of Fury was totally true!

How had he got himself into this terrible situation? Would he ever be free again? What would happen? What does the wicked creature want from him? As all these thoughts race through his mind, he cries and shouts for help. But the more he wiggles, the tighter the veil envelops him, while his screams are drowned out by the buzzing wasps.

He listens to the song of the fearsome Queen. She is praising herself for kidnapping a new victim.

"I'll scratch and bite her. I hate her. I'll kick and hit." To his despair, the red veil's grip just gets tighter and tighter, and the red heat more and more intense.

"Nearly there, my lovely," the Queen hisses in a scary voice. "Nearly there. It is great. You are one of the angriest boys I have ever captured. That will keep me going for a bit. Harr-harr-harr. Don't calm down!"

Soon afterwards they land in a strange place. Philip cannot see very much through the veil. But it appears they flew through a kind of green curtain that magically parted on entry. "Leaves?" he thinks with astonishment.

The ride ends with a bump as he lands on some hard soil.

Through some strands of red material he can just make out an enormous green roof that arches all the way down to the ground. Daylight filters through it.

"Harr-harr-harr! My dear little boy. You think you can escape from here? You will have to think again. We have arrived as guests, harr-harr-harr, of my ally, the almighty weeping willow. Harr-harr. His branches follow my command. It's the world's most secure cage!"

Philip realises it is a tree the Queen is talking about. He thinks he has seen it before on his walks through the park. It stands at a fork of two paths. He has never told anyone about it, but he has secretly always been a bit scared of that tree. It has a very dense curtain of knife shaped leaves, so once you enter you feel like you are cut off from the outside world. The long arms of the branches close immediately, leaving you all alone, facing the tree trunk. As you look up, you can make out the bark, all gnarled and crinkled. In its shadows you can see shapes resembling an old man's face looking down at you in a very serious, almost frightening way. Not a friendly face. A wizard?

All the kids went in there to play. It's that sort of place where you shudder a bit, but in a nice way. Like at Halloween, when you meet a ghost. Even though you know it is only some kid you probably know, it is still a bit eerie.

Little do all these children know that in the case of this tree, it is truly haunted. The spirit of the tree is ruled by the wicked Queen of Fury.

"Let me out, let me out!" Philip shouts and tries to free himself from the hold of the veil. "It is only a tree! You can't scare me."

He gets more and more angry.

The heat intensifies again.

"Yes, you are a brilliant find! Keep going, keep going. You make me stronger and stronger."

He surely is trapped. He tries to remember what Anna had told him; something about the fury, the anger. That was it, that was the key. "The angrier I get, the stronger the red hot veil gets. But how can I not be angry?"

Anger is Philip's best way to get anything in life. Throwing a fit usually gets his mum to do something to calm him down. The only thing that he's not got through aggression is his friendship with Anna. But now?

Wouldn't she now be mad with him?

He suddenly feels very sad. He was the one who had messed it all up. Anna had been so good to him. She had taken him to her secret world.

"What a stupid boy I am. I will have lost her trust, even if I ever make it out of here."

His anger disappears, instead a feeling of deep gloom overpowers him.

He feels the space around him cooling down, and to his surprise, the hold of the veil lessens. He is able to push it away.

Strange noises come from the Queen. She gurgles: "No, no my friend. Come on. You are my best prey. My slave. You are so good at being angry. Don't stop now." And then in a shrill voice cries: "I command you!"

At that, Philip thinks: "How dare she? I am not her slave. Stupid!" And, of course, some anger naturally wells up in him.

Promptly the heat and the grip of the veil are back and he once again can't move anymore.

"Good, angry boy. I knew it. You are brilliant!"

Philip begins to understand: the angrier he gets, the stronger her hold on him. He must find a way to calm himself down. It's his only chance of rescue!

He thinks of Anna's face when she was telling him all about her adventures with the strange creatures. She had looked so nice. Her cheeks slightly flushed, her face very animated. Thinking of this helps him to regain control of his anger. He is focused on his resolution. "Calm, calm." Will it work?

The first thing that weakens is the heat, and then the veil changes colour, from the really tomato kind of red to a pink, and then a washed out foggy grey. Next it is developing big holes. And, as he watches in fascination, it finally pops into nothingness, just like soap bubbles do when they burst in the air.

And again he is free to move!

"I will be getting out of here," he says aloud and walks over to the green leaf curtain. But when he tries to push his way though the dense foliage, he finds the branches react like tentacles of a strange sea creature. They grab him, trip him and push him back. The extremely hard, sharp-edged leaves cut into his fingers.

"Well, you might think you're being clever, harr-harr. But you did not count on the powers that my dear friend, the Green Man, and I have over you, harr-harr! Keep trying you little creature. It might get you nice and angry again!"

Her wicked horrible laughter echoes through his head.

"There is no escape from our fangs for naughty little boys!"

Philip is petrified. How can he get out of here? He can't see any way to escape. However, by using all his willpower, he tries not to be provoked into anger again. He suddenly realises how exhausted he has become. The wicked Queen has fed on his energy well. He looks down at his hands. They hurt. A small trickle of blood has now dried where the leaves have cut his fingers. He sits down on the hard ground and puts his head down onto his knees. There is nobody to witness his crying.

ASSEMBLY

Oscar is in charge of making sure the whole community gets to hear the terrible news.

His thin but very strong legs drum the ground. Fortunately, it hadn't rained for a while so it is nice and firm. His message is drummed out in a rhythm resembling the Morse code that was once used on old ships. It will then be decoded by the moles and others into the following: "Danger, Danger! The old enemy, the Queen of Fury, is back in our land. She has kidnapped a friend of one of the Chosen. All on red alert! Message over."

Whilst Anna is watching Oscar, she notices whole armies of ants coming from everywhere, joining the drumming as the message gets repeated over and over.

Next, the ground around them starts to move. An earthquake? She realises that, instead, it is caused by a number of molehills appearing all around the hollow where Toady has her headquarters. Mrs Toad tells the moles to call everybody for an assembly. They look funny as they all jump back into their tunnels to rush out the latest message.

Under Oscar's command, the ants are organised into a land transport system for the slower members of the community.

The space in front of the old oak tree soon gets very crowded as it fills with a huge variety of creatures.

Most of them are animals – insects, birds, rodents, small mammals – but there are also a few chestnut people riding in, not all Scottish. It is quite a spectacle.

Anna manages to spot Woody Woodborer, still wearing his apron. He must have been in the middle of baking. Next to him is Mrs Owl; she probably flew him there. Then there are two cute looking squirrels, a number of grasshoppers, some bees, a duck, a moorhen, four gulls, a number of different butterflies, caterpillars and some woodlice.

Anna feels slightly dizzy as she is trying to make out individual members of this colourful crowd.

Mrs Toad has climbed up onto a molehill and is addressing everyone.

She croaks to clear her throat and then starts with: "Quiet, please, everybody."

They all react instantly and turn their attention to their boss.

"I am grateful to all of you to have responded to our emergency call so promptly. Even though it very inconvenient for you, I felt it was a matter of upmost urgency to call you all to this general assembly. Our peace is in great danger. Our boundaries have been intruded by the Queen of Fury and some of her followers. I will now give you a brief summary of the unfortunate events that have happened today."

In her briefing, she talks about Philip, his kidnap and how it came about. All the time she does not once blame Anna for bringing him down with her. On the contrary, she takes full responsibility for allowing her to do so.

"Let us not fall into lamentations and dwell on feeling sorry for ourselves. What we need to have now is quick action! As long as the Queen has her hold over the poor boy, she can grow stronger and more powerful. Already she has managed to enslave a swarm of wasps into her service. It was made angry by some human chasing them away from a litter bin with his walking stick. This anger, as we all know, is welcome fodder for the horrible Queen. So, all of us must exercise control over our tempers to the highest degree! In case you feel in danger of losing it, please take some of the cream. The ants have been busy producing it right now for the possible high demand there may be in this emergency. We are all just creatures in the end, we all have our weaknesses."

Anna feels her back pocket. The crumbled dry leaf is still there, but she had better get a fresh supply. She regrets that she was not able to give some to Philip.

"We need to find a way to free the boy. It will be a dangerous and difficult task. I have been informed that he is being held captive under the weeping willow. She has managed to get a strong hold over his spirit, the Green Man."

They hear Otto shout: "Oh no, not the Green Man! He is such an unpredictable feller. Jinks. You know he is perfectly reasonable and friendly when the spring comes, especially in May. But later in the growing season, when his foliage gets denser, he becomes very withdrawn and angry. Nobody quite understands why. Maybe it's because some kids hurt him and make him angry by pulling on his branches to swing on them. That would get him furious and you know, with the Queen and all..."

Anna and some of the others shudder when they hear Mrs Owl saying the next bit: "Let's assess the scenario as follows: the Queen, the wasps and the Green Man form a nearly invincible trio. Their strategy is to keep Philip really angry till he loses strength. It does not bear thinking about what will happen then. It is a vicious circle. He can't help it. Even if he realises he has to overcome his anger to free himself from her grip, one of them will do something to stir it up again. The wasps might start stinging him to achieve this. Unlike bees, they don't risk anything by doing this. I really, really fear for the boy. Apart from that, there is naturally the danger to our well-being through her intrusion. We must come up with a plan. Any ideas and suggestions?"

There are lots of volunteers who want to enter the tree's canopy and take the boy out. They are willing to sacrifice a lot for their community. But the wise toad just shakes her head to all the ideas so far. They won't work, either because they are too dangerous or just impossible.

The moles come up with a plan. They'll dig a tunnel to the boy, then the ants can come and protect him with their cream and carry him to safety.

After some exploratory tunnelling they return, quite exhausted after the effort. But it's all in vain. The ground is so hard, it is just like concrete. They can't get through.

The ducks come up with a suggestion. They could bring water in their beaks, and by other means, to flood the area and soften the ground. But they all realise that it would alert the Green Man because willow trees have a very acute sense for water.

The ants feel that an organised military attack might be the answer. They could form lines armed with the long needles from Scotch pine trees. Because of their slender size, they would be able to squeeze through the tiny spaces between the leaves and branches.

But Mrs Toad warns them that: "This is the sort of thing they might have been setting up as a trap for us! Someone might get angry and that will lead to even more victims and the triumph of the Fury Queen!"

Eventually, it is Rat who comes up with a brilliant plan. He has been sitting quietly listening to the others. Anna has watched him because he keeps scratching his scraggly head. She wonders if it is fleas that cause him to be restless. Secretly, she fears that she'll catch some herself, which isn't funny, the size she is at present!

As it turns out, it will be these very fleas that form an essential part of rat's intelligent operation.

He finally gets to talk: "I suggest that we analyse things a bit, my dear friends. May, is it. May, you said Mrs Toad, is the month when the Green Man is in his most favourable mood?" he asks politely.

"Yes, indeed it is. There is no real explanation for this. Nobody knows much about the Green Man."

"Well, I do wonder," says Rat, scratching his head again. "Maybe it is to do with humans again, like so many things." He turns to Anna. "Dear, have you any idea what May is famous for?"

Anna blushes as she suddenly finds herself the centre of attention.

She replies cautiously: "I am sorry, but I am very bad at remembering the names of the months and when they are. But is May not the month when there is lots of dancing going on? Isn't it the first of May when, early in the morning, a children's choir sings from the roof of that big tower over there?"

Rat says: "Yes, Anna, that is right, now that you say it. It is a great morning. Usually so busy in town and in the park as well with lots of lovely half-empty crisp packets, pizza cartons and lots for me to feast on! Any idea what they are celebrating?"

"I have never really been out much for that. But once we had visitors from the States, and they and their kids dragged us all out early in the morning for the choir singing. There were also lots of things going on. Mum said it was to celebrate the arrival of spring. Happy stuff. The winter is gone and everything grows and so on. There was so much music everywhere, I loved it. There were some funny men all dressed in white, with stockings with bells on. They were jumping and dancing, making music and clicking some sticks. Weird, but nice too."

"That's it, that's it!" Rat shouts with excitement. "The Green Man loves music, singing and dancing. It's the time when his tree grows stronger. My family and I once watched him on that morning. He responded to the music and dancing. Looked as if his branches were dancing too. There was only a soft breeze, no real wind at all. They were waving in all sorts of directions and his face, when you saw it, was actually really happy looking for a change!"

Rat points with his finger to his forehead: "Yes, that'll be the plan. Let's pretend it is May. Stage the whole scenario. Make him happy!"

Immediately, he gets into organising mode: "We need some musicians, some singers and, of course, some dancers. We'll start the concert with a soft melody. Gradually, we'll build it up, getting louder and louder. We have to learn some of those songs. The praises of nature. Can you teach us, Anna?"

"Yes, I think I can teach you some songs."

Rat carries on: "Hopefully, this will change his mood. He'll be confused but start believing it's spring again. The wicked Queen will start losing her hold over the Green Man."

He laughs: "I'll lend you my little troop of fleas. They are fantastic dancers. Waltzes and all. Hopping mad at times, I say."

"I see," says Mrs Toad. "What a cunning idea! Then he'll start dancing, waving his branches. That will clear a path into the space under the willow. Yes, I can see that would work."

"Yes," Rat keenly adds. "Someone will have to be brave and grab the child and bring him to safety. Anna your job will be to keep him calm. To tell him not to get angry. Make him realise that he has to help. And how to apply the cream, just in case. We need to weaken the Queen."

"What about the wasps?" one of the squirrels asks.

"A very good question. But I have thought about that too. We need to lure the wasps away.

Otherwise, their stings might make Philip or his rescuer angry, we can't afford to take that risk."

"My parents have a wasp trap in our garden. It is a kind of glass thing with some sugar water in it. Then the wasps want the sugar and crawl in, but can't get out," Anna says, but suddenly goes really red in the face. "Sorry, not nice I know. But we are quite scared of the stings, you know."

"Not to worry too much. The wasps are funny creatures. At the end of the summer they have real anger issues. They very often become victims of the Queen. So we do understand. Her threads of anger lead them like puppets on a string. They obey and serve her blindly." It is the gentle voice of Isy Owl explaining.

Rat says: "What a splendid idea. I know just the thing! I spent last night in that super bin over there. There was a great spread of delicacies in there, by the way. Cheese from sandwiches, crisps, apples oh, so many lovely foods."

He licks his lips before he carries on: "But there are also some cans. Drink cans. They usually have a bit left in them, enough for the likes of us to wash everything down, whilst sitting there on a balmy evening. Yum, watching the world go by and having a little drink. That's the life! Mustn't get carried away. Stay focused," he apologises.

"I'll just nip over and bring one with a really nice sugary drink. I'll roll it to the tree. As soon as the wasps smell the sugar, they'll go for it!"

Mrs Toad looks at Rat with admiration and says: "Well, Rudi Rat. I always knew you had some brains between those ears. I think you have just come up with a remarkable plan. It certainly will give us a chance."

The grasshoppers put their little arms up to get attention. One of them suggests: "We don't want to sing our own praises, hah, figure of speech. But you know, we are good musicians. It would be an honour to be involved."

"Yes, let's start recruiting. We will need singers? Anyone?" There are lots of good voices coming forward. Anna is put in charge of the choir, as she suggests we make up the songs in a way that will tell Philip what is happening.

After the auditions, Anna has taken on the bumblebees for the humming, some frogs for the deep voices and the gulls for volume, among others.

As squirrels are such great runners, they are recruited to do the rescue run under the tree. To find out the fastest, they immediately start a race.

Anna is pleased with her choice of singers. The gulls are great at keeping a tune and certainly loud enough. Despite all the horror of this situation, a strange kind of party mood has started. Everyone is glad that they can do something, and not just sit around and worry.

After sufficient practice, organisation and learning, they are finally ready to have a go.

It is a strange procession that sets off on the path in the direction of the weeping willow.

First there's Mrs Toad, followed closely by Rudi Rat, who is rolling a can of very sweet lemonade in front of him. Some very strong black beetles are lending a hand.

Next follows the grasshoppers. Dressed for the occasion in tails and bowties, they carefully carry their violins.

Then it is Anna and her choir.

The excited squirrels keep running off to the sides, only to then return to their positions in the procession. They have now decided who is to run. The other one will be on standby, just in case. Deep in their furry pockets, they carry some anti-anger cream to apply to Philip.

Like soldiers, the ants accompany the troop, ready to supply their cream if needed. Some are slowed down slightly as they are giving Otto and his friends and family an easy ride.

There is still a long tail of all the other creatures following on behind. Nobody wants to miss the event. They are all ready for action – in case they're needed in the rescue operation.

THE RESCUE

The willow is enormous. It towers like a gigantic green dome in front of the group. Its branches are trailing all the way down to the ground. The knife shaped leaves are so close to each other it is impossible to look through them to catch a glimpse of the trapped boy.

Anna's heart is gripped by cold fear. She is shivering.

As if saying a prayer, she begs that things will work out alright for her friend, Philip.

She is not sure whether it is an illusion, an image made up by her own mind, or if she really can see some fibre-like red strands underneath the ends of some of the branches.

She remembers when the red hot veil covered her, closing tightly around her with an invisible grip, and her incredible rage as she bit into Amanda's back. That wicked creature, the Queen, who's living – well, thriving – on her anger! She has goosebumps all over her skin.

"Concentration. Don't get provoked or else she'll find more victims!" she tells herself. "I must get that message through to Philip, so that he understands the Queen's workings."

They are all gathered now in front of the willow, forming a large semi-circle.

Oscar walks over after he has let Otto climb down from his back first. He rubs the squirrels, Henry and William, almost completely in the ant's anti-anger cream. They look quite shiny. Henry will enter the space, and William is the back up.

Rudi Rat carefully positions the drinks can in such a way that its opening faces the tree. Next, he pours some of the sticky lemonade out. That way, it will smell stronger and the trail will attract the wasps. Lovely sweet smells are building up already in the warm sunshine.

Mrs Toad is the conductor. Everybody is waiting for her to give the signal to start the concert. Anna fixes her eyes on her, while her heart beats so hard, she is convinced the others can hear it.

There goes the sign. A gentle melody fills the air. Anna now joins in with her choir. She sings as loud and clear as possible. A beautiful song, all about nature and beauty, with some lines aimed at Philip mixed in. He has to understand that this is the beginning of his rescue.

Will he understand? "We stand by you... Love is in the air... You are not alone... Stay calm..." These are some of the songs. She hopes some of the words that have been built in will reach him. Should she be more open? But she does not want the Queen to understand what is going on, as there is always the danger she might spoil it by telling the tree.

Rudi Rat is in charge of the dancing fleas. They look hilariously gorgeous as they hop up and down in the required fashion. They are waving little white handkerchiefs in their hands and jingling tiny bells that are fitted to their lower legs.

The singing and the instruments are now filling the air with fabulous music. Soon, they all become aware of a slight movement in the tree. Not much, it is barely noticeable, but it's enough to encourage more singing and playing. The tunes sound even merrier. The dancing is frantic!

Is it going to work?

There:

A shudder is going through the whole tree.

Like a sudden gust of wind, the branches are swaying. They no longer resemble tentacles. They rather look like very long arms waving their green leaves like the handkerchiefs of the small hopping fleas.

The motion of the dancing branches stirs the air sufficiently to bring the scent of the lemonade over to the wasps. The crowd of spectators watch with fascination as first one, then two, then three and finally dozens and dozens of wasps crawl and fly out straight for the tin, fighting for space as they clamber inside. Greed is getting the better of them as they crowd deeper into the dark space of the can. It soon becomes almost impossible to get back out.

A strange sight begins to appear. The Red Queen is still trying to hold onto her reins to restrain and direct the wasps, but in her efforts, she has been pulled flat onto her stomach and dragged over towards the can. All the time, she is throwing some red anger strands over towards the wasps; a thing that normally works to get them really on attack mode. But this time the lure of the strong sugar smell proves stronger, and the wasps head straight for their prison.

To make sure they definitively stay in there, Rat now rushes over and plugs the hole with a stone he has ready for that purpose. He looks the Queen straight in the eyes, laughing at the sight of her.

The strange scene is still filled with the music and the first goal has been achieved. Now they have to make sure the Queen does not regain control of the Green Man.

Their joint efforts keep going. The music gets louder and more tuneful than ever, with the violins leading a fast and happy fiddle song, to which the fleas outperform themselves in jumping even higher and higher. As if touched by magic, the tree is following their example and sways its branches right up into the air.

The Queen, still lying on her belly, turns her head round and shouts: "You silly old fool. You stupid numpkin! What do you think you are doing?"

Totally ignoring her, the branches of the tree swing more and more.

This is the moment for Henry the squirrel. The green curtain has parted and they all can now see Philip's astonished face as he tries to stand up from his cowering position. Anna is relieved to see that he seems to have understood the messages. There is certainly no sign of anger in his face. Rather the opposite. He looks hopeful and almost happy, but also totally exhausted. A faint smile steels into his face as he looks at the Queen on her belly and the hopping fleas.

Anna keeps singing as she watches Henry. He is checking all around him. Squirrels have great vision, they can spot danger very early.

Quick as a flash of lightning, he shoots under the tree, tries to grab Philip and –

A horrible scream fills the air.

It is Henry. In his race to get to the poor frightened boy, he had not seen that one of the wasps had become entangled in a thread from the veil. The yellow and black insect has stung him in the softest part of his foot when he stepped on it, and the pain is excruciating.

"Harr-harr-harr!" The sound of the Queen's triumphant laughter can be heard over the music as the evil creature throws red hot veil strands right over poor Henry.

But the strands just fall off him, as if he has a glass dome over him. The anti-anger cream that Oscar has applied to Henry in wise anticipation is working well to protect him.

"What is wrong with you, you silly old man? Are you totally off your rocker?" she shouts at the Green Man's face, who has changed from someone really scary that gives you the creeps to looking like a proud Granddad listening to your solo in a school performance.

"You idiot! You old idiot! You are not falling for that usual soppy rubbish again? That can't be true. Damn. Close your branches! I say, close your branches!" But the old tree just ignores her. While her shrill voice shouts her commands, he keeps on happily swaying his branches to the rhythm.

William, the other squirrel, has been watching what has happened and responds in no time at all. Running in with lightning speed, he swoops Philip up and carries him to safety. Poor Henry is limping behind them.

Philip looks pale and tired.

The same can be said for the Queen. She is losing her strength very quickly. One angry wasp is not enough to keep her going for long. She has wasted her energy with all the shouting and screaming, and her grip is now weakening. Even the one wasp that is left starts crawling over to the spilled lemonade and is very happy to get as much sugary syrup into itself as possible.

The crowd is breaking out into a spontaneous round of applause as the beaten Queen flies off in a faint pink cloud, that is now almost grey, with lots of holes in it. She is in search of better victims in some other place.

Anna rushes over to Philip as soon as he is gently lowered down by William. She gives him a very strong bear hug. Her relief is tremendous. Again, all the onlookers are clapping their paws, hands, wings or whatever they can use.

Only the tree is starting to look a bit sad. "Is that it? Is the first of May over again?" He does not want to go back to his usual grumpy mood.

One of the ants is alert and spots the change in the Green Man's expression. He rushes over and starts rubbing some of the anti-anger cream on some of his leaves, which by now are hanging down in the usual way that gives the weeping willow its name.

It has the desired effect of fending off the anger, but the old tree's face still looks quite sad. Some of the crickets realise what is going on and start promptly playing their soft violin. They promise the tree to do this from now on every evening in the summer.

By now, Philip is so exhausted from his horrible ordeal, he is barely able to stand up on his own two legs. Anna is still holding onto his arm.

Isy Owl walks over to the two reunited friends. She gently stokes the boy with one of her soft wing feathers over his cheek and says: "Dear, oh dear. You poor old thing. The wicked Queen nearly had your energy completely. We got you just in time, I think. It would be such a good idea to spend a couple of nights in our cocoon hammocks. But I don't want your parents to start a search through the park. It would scare your poor mother too much. So we'd better leave that for a bit. But I have the impression that you are far too weak to ride the rainbow spiral back. So, Anna, I am afraid you'd better make your return by yourself. Mole will take you back to Otto's. Is that OK for you?"

"Sure, yeah, I'll be fine. But what about Philip. How is he going to return?" Anna asks in a concerned voice.

At that, the owl opens up her wing and wraps it round the boys back in a gentle embrace. "Philip, you poor little thing, you look so washed out. I will make a special exception for you. Ever been airlifted by an owl before? I'll take you and fly you home."

Philip, even though he is so tired, manages to whisper: "Cool," as he is invited to climb onto the broad back of the old bird.

In the unique way that owls can turn their head right round, she looks at him as he holds on and promises him: "In a few days I'll send you my bat mobile to bring you back for that dream treat in my hammock. You'll sleep the best sleep you've ever had under those softly spun blankets, your head on the cocoon pillow. You will feel loved and wanted. It'll help you to cope with the Queen better – oh, dear, better get going. Make sure you don't roll off."

Her soothing voice has started to put Philip to sleep before she has had the chance to lift of. For a moment, he is able to raise his head a tiny bit again, just to see everyone getting smaller and smaller, waving a big farewell to him.

Before Anna follows the mole, who is now beckoning to her, she turns round to thank everyone for all their efforts to help, and to apologise again for having been involved in creating the dangerous situation they had fortunately been able to fend off.

"Aye, lassie, no worries, you weren't to know. Not your fault." Otto is looking at her. "We should have known better, but no harm done in the end. Lessons learned, that's the main thing."

Henry, the injured squirrel, grins at her: "You look after yourself now. Look what great things I'm getting out of it." He points to Woody Woodborer, who is rubbing a lovely scented oil into his poor foot. He is clearly enjoying the massage.

She realises what a great group of friends they all are to each other, including her; the best friends she has ever had.

She waves at them as she follows Mole.

AT PHILIP'S HOUSE

The flight of the owl is completely silent. Soon the trees and bushes of the park change into an elegant urban landscape. The brick houses in the area where Philip and Anna live are enormous, normally two or three stories high with big bay windows. There are front and back gardens. From the street, there are wide drives that are entered through gates left open so that the cars can return home without the owner bothering to open them.

Philip's dad works very hard, long hours. "Money does not grow on trees." His mum is able to stay at home and look after all of them. The house and the garden take up a lot of her time. Then there are the school runs, of course, and activities for the children. She feels very lucky. Not many of her friends are able to be full-time mums.

Sometimes, she gets a bit lonely. That's why she does some volunteering, like when she comes to help with the reading in her daughter's class. She would never dare to do the same in Philip's. That would be so embarrassing for her, the way he behaves.

"I don't know why he is so wild," she often thinks. "We look after them so well. They have everything

I never had. All because their dad works so hard. For all of us."

She thinks back to her own childhood. They had only one bathroom, and that had the loo in as well! Her mum worked In a shoe shop! She fitted all the children's shoes. She also made them giggle and allowed them to ride on the rocking horse in the shop. Dad looked after some colleges. That way he worked his hours, so that there was always someone at home for her and her two brothers. Their garden didn't have the beautiful roses she has now. Instead, it had an old and creaky swing, some rabbits in a hutch and a veggie plot. It was very useful and always cared for by all of them. She sighs. Had the sun shone so much more when she had been a little girl?

She likes to spoil her children. Jack always blames her for Philip's behaviour. It is probably her fault, he must be right.

It is so bad. Usually caused by... well, nobody really knows. It's all Philip, of course. He is so angry. Then Jack flips, and then... well, she does not want to think about it. Her dad had never really hit his children. He had probably been too soft. Jack must know. He deals with all sorts of kids in his job as a hospital doctor. Jack can't help his temper, he gets provoked by the boy, the poor man. Never at work, of course.

He really does not want to hit anyone. Not Philip, definitively not. He is his son. He loves him.

It's not his fault and he is so sad afterwards. Cries sometimes as well. Just as well Philip's sister is such an angel. The total opposite. She must take after dad, all bright and sparkly.

Philip's mum breathes in deeply as she gazes out of the big bay window.

What was that, an owl in the middle of the day? She must be seeing things. Owls don't fly around in the afternoon, they are night birds.

"Dear, dear, you are starting to imagine things. Not good. Better get busy with dinner."

She loves cooking in her massive kitchen. It has an island in the middle for sitting at and chatting. Not that anyone really does chat these days. There's not much entertaining and socialising. Not since they had moved here.

She had not really wanted to move, but Jack was right, the house is in the top location and much bigger. In the old one, there had been neighbours popping in, just so. The kids playing in the gardens or even in the streets! But yes, the kids' rooms were small. And the people living here, well they are much more the type they should be friends with. Jack is right, as usual.

It is so close to the right schools as well. Not that Philip will get into one, but –

Her thoughts are cut short by a strange noise on the stairs outside the front entrance, a kind of scratchy noise.

"Burglars!" she thinks as fear shoots through her body. She has not put any lights on and it looks like nobody's home from the outside. "Oh no, what to do?"

She is scared as she listens again. Is that someone's voice?

Her senses become very acute. There is definitely something or someone. Should she dial 999 and call the police?

She is shaky as she tiptoes to the other window to secretly look out and see what is happening, her mobile in her hand, ready to dial.

All she can make out from this angle is a shape of a familiar looking trainer. "Philip's?"

She cranes her neck, and yes, she is able to see the foot in the trainer and the bottom end of one of Philip's legs.

"My God!" she shouts, running to open the door. What has happened, why is he lying there? Is he hurt, stabbed?

She runs out as quickly as she can, her heart beating right up into her neck.

She bends over him. He is sprawled out over the entrance area, his head leaning against the bottom bar of the railing.

He looks a deadly pale colour.

"Oh Philip! My goodness. What is wrong? What has happened? Have you been in a fight? Has someone done something to you? Answer, please. For goodness sake, please say something."

Philip just stares up at his mother. His big brown eyes are wide open, as if he has seen a ghost.

"Phipsie, come on Phipsie, sweetheart. What is the matter?" His mum has not called him that name for a long time. She used to, when he was little. It was his baby name. She keeps whispering this name while she is gently picking him up to carry him inside. A small soft feather is stirring on the front step.

He is quite big and heavy now, but she manages and puts him down gently on the red sofa in the entrance hall.

She used to be a nurse, that's how she had met her husband. He had already been a great doctor and a bit older. She had loved nursing, but stopped working to look after her children.

She has not forgotten her training, however, and so can check Philip over immediately. She feels his forehead, no, there's no temperature. His pulse is regular but quite slow and weak. As a matter of fact, the whole boy seems to be totally weak. Drained of energy, he is all limp and just stares at his mother.

"He is not a bad boy," she thinks. "He is my baby." She loves him so much, but does not like to show it too often. It would spoil him too much. But now: she looks at him. He is so poorly, but she can't see any injuries or fresh bruises

Kissing him gently on the top of his head, she pleads: "Poor darling, I wish you would tell me what is wrong," but he just keeps staring.

"I'll just take you upstairs to bed. Make you nice and cosy. Your sister, Angelina, is not here, she is at Jessie's for supper. So I will make you a nice cup of hot chocolate and then sit beside you till you are ready to tell me. How does that sound?"

She carries him upstairs. She is quite fit as she works out in the gym. She looks at his bedroom as they enter, it's such a fabulous room.

Brilliant computer, all the games, a Wii, remote car and boat for the pond – everything a boy could dream of. Why is he never happy? Nobody understands. That's what makes Jack angry sometimes. He gives the boy so much. They both are puzzled about Philip's outbursts. His behaviour can be so unpredictable. It's all nice and happy and then: boom! Out of the blue, he shouts, kicks things and slams the door shut. Eventually, his Dad reacts and slaps him. Not surprising. Wrong, they know, but what can they do?

She pushes these thoughts away as she looks at him leaning his head against her, just like a baby.

She gently lowers him down onto his bed and starts taking his jeans and tops of. It's such a long time since she has done that.

He looks quite skinny.

She spots some old bruises on his lower back. They look like finger marks. Big fingers.

"Things have to change." A smack is a smack, but this has gone too far. She has to be strong and stand up for Philip. They both love him. How can the parents stop what's happening?

At that a little smile appears on Philip's face and he turns towards his mum saying: "Thanks, Mum. I am just sooo tired. I just want to sleep. Sorry, it's so nice that you promised me a hot chocolate, but I don't think I can manage it," he yawns. "Mum, before you go out, could you open the window a little bit, please? And don't leave the door open, I think I sleep better with it closed. Thanks mum," he says, unable to keep his eyes open any longer.

"What is that about," she thinks. Both kids leave the door open all the time, especially when they are in bed. They feel safer with the landing light on at night.

"Well, he is growing up a bit. It would be better to leave it for my discussion with Jack later anyway, in case voices get raised."

She plants a small kiss on his forehead, and before she is out of the room, Philip is fast asleep.

Those bruises look horrible. She can't get them out of her mind. Just as well they are in a place where nobody at school would spot them.

She goes downstairs and phones the house of her daughter's friend. She asks them if they would mind if Angelina slept over for the night. The girls like doing that as often as they can. They're not normally allowed to do so during the week. She explains that Philip is not well and it might, therefore, be a good idea to keep brother and sister apart, just in case It was infectious.

While preparing dinner, she keeps thinking of what to do about Philip. How she and Jack should react to his outbursts.

"I think it is wrong to get so angry about him," she tells Jack later after she's described how she has carried Philip in after he collapsed at the front door, and then saw some finger marks on his back.

"Hitting is not right. We are the adults, after all."

Philip's Dad feels very embarrassed. His face is all flushed when he explains: "I don't know what came over me. He was just so, so... I can't even say. I just lost it. He kept making me angry. I just, well, I am not proud of it. Will he ever forgive me?"

Little does he know about the wicked and evil Queen of Fury and what a strong hold she held over their son. How she loved those wild outbursts of his, and put her strands of anger all over the boy. And even better, watched as the father became a victim too. She needed humans like them, who are nice and easy to get into temper fits.

Philip sleeps one of the deepest sleeps he has ever had, full of dreams. There are little fleas dancing and hopping, crickets playing tunes on violins, gulls singing and – a very pretty girl smiling at him!

But best of all, he relives Mrs Owl's airlift. That was just so brilliant. She had whispered a reminder to him to leave the window of his bedroom open and the door shut, as she dropped him off, so his parents would get used to it. She promised him a mobile bat soon. He had felt a weird sensation when she had put him down in front of the house. It felt almost like growing pains as he regained his normal size. Weird.

Then she had scratched at the door to his house with her claws before silently fling off, back to the park.

BACK IN GRACE

When Anna is back in school, she gets told to go and see the head in her office again.

"Oh my God," she feels really scared. "What is it this time? What have I done?"

She can't remember doing anything, but of course, she has a bad conscience. There must have been something.

She knocks with some hesitation on the door.

"Come in." Anna does not really want to. Her knees are a bit wobbly. She's so silly.

But Anna slowly pushes the door handle down and enters.

Mrs Bingfield resides, as usual, behind her enormous desk with her computer switched on, showing lots of different columns. She had been working on the duty rota.

She is a scary looking person. Her hair is very curly and very red; the kind of red that older ladies often have. She obviously loves gold and jewellery a lot. Gold-rimmed spectacles are dangling down from a golden chain onto her mountainous breasts. Her wrinkly neck is nearly strangled by three tiers of pearls. Her curved fingers are crowned with massive rings, their glittering stones reflecting the light of the computer screen. 'Like claws with long red nails,' Anna thinks.

Like the witch in Hansel and Gretel, her curved finger motions Anna to come further towards her. Thick lipstick in a matching tone has left a few traces on her yellow teeth, which she now exposes with her fake smile.

"Sit down, my dear, sit down," she says "Now Anna. What do you have to say for yourself? How are things turning out now? Any change? How is your behaviour? Any improvements?" She snorts a funny little laugh through her bulbous nose, which is decorated with a tiny hairy wart on one nostril.

"Well, child, speak! Speak."

Anna hasn't a clue what is expected of her. She stutters: "I don't know, Miss. I, eh, eh, don't think I done anything wrong."

"I have done," the headmistress corrects sternly. "I have done. Please speak properly."

"Sorry, Miss. I have done. No, I mean, I have not done, I eh, hem." She gets very confused.

"But if you think, Miss, I have. You know I don't mind the library for longer. Not that much. Keeps me out of trouble. If you know what I mean?"

"Well, well. Could there be a tiny bit of hope on the horizon? A little improvement by any chance?" she snorts again.

"Actually, young lady. I think we have done quite the right thing for you there. I hear that you obviously have benefitted from the attention of my dear colleagues. Mrs James is very capable, and nice and strict. I am sure it is mainly down to

her that your writing skills have improved a lot."
She stares at Anna.

After a pause she continues: "Well done, I have said to her. To teach the unteachable. Well done. What an achievement!"

Anna looks back at her smug face. She is not betraying her secret.

'The unteachable.' So, that's what they think of me. Not very nice. Maybe I should call her, and her like, the un-teachers? Never mind,' she says to herself. Still, it does hurt a bit. She is not unteachable! Obviously.

She feels a familiar heat rising up her neck. 'No,' she quickly tells herself. 'No, don't give the wicked Queen a chance.'

She calms herself down enough to look at the old teacher.

"Well, I tell you that we have held a lot of class councils about you. With a lot of hesitation, we've all agreed to give you a chance after all. You shall be allowed to rejoin your classmates on the playground again after lunch. But before you go 'hooray' and think it's all forgiven and over, I must warn you: you will be constantly monitored for bad behaviour. You'll have a behaviour diary that you'll have to present to the duty teacher at the end of every playtime to track any mishaps. More than one, and you'll go back onto detention."

She looks down at Anna. "Do you understand me? If you do anything nasty, hit or pull hair or so, the privileges will be stopped immediately. I have some doubts, but hope you will prove me wrong by behaving well. You will still go into the library during the other break times to benefit from the excellent teaching of my dear colleague, Mrs James, whose rota I have changed specially, so that you get her all the time. We go through a lot of effort for you, my dear."

Spit threads are spanning her open mouth as she speaks. So disgusting.

"Dismissed. Go back to class!" She shoos her away as if she was a bluebottle fly on her desk.

"Thank you, Miss, thank you. That is good news," Anna lies politely before she leaves.

She should be happy. She can play with her friends again. Friends, what friends? Of course, there is Philip. He stayed at home today. But you can't possibly be seen with a boy too much, especially an older one.

"Anna is in lohove, haha, Anna is in lohove." They will chant. They might tempt her to use her fists again. No, it's better to see him outside school hours. Anyway, no way. She is definitely not. Not in love. Just friendship.

Anna feels very alone as she enters the playground for the first time after her punishment.

Everybody seems busy. Running, hopping on the squares and skipping ropes – the long ones where you chant whilst jumping over the rope with two girls turning it. Or some short ones. Some kids have stilts. Looks quite good fun. They have really nice things to keep them active in the playground in her school. She knows that children don't get that everywhere. Her cousin is really jealous.

It is quite loud. She's never noticed that before. The library has made her ears sensitive.

She walks around in search of some group that she can join in. But she feels quite weird. She has never suffered a shortage of friends before, always been a really sociable girl.

She keeps walking around. Normally someone would say: "Hey there is Anna. You're joining, please, we need another one." For tag, definitely. She is so fast. But there is no one she usually hangs around with.

She stands and watches a group that's playing with marbles, the latest craze. It's not really her thing. Not wild enough. But it looks quite interesting. They get quite heated about the different values and who's won what. But suddenly she's told: "Push off! Stop staring! Moron. You give us the creeps." A round of angry eyes is fixed on her.

"Sor – ry!" Anna says and walks away. She does not dare to reply to the provocation. No trouble, thanks!

Well, there are always the crossbars. She slowly walks over. She can always just do her turns. Hasn't done any in ages. Damn. There is an older girl already at the top one.

Anna has to settle for the lower one. It's not so easy to spin fast. She is too tall. She decides to just sit on it and look out. She has a better view from there.

"Where on earth is Emma?" she says to herself.

"Ah, there she is." She has spotted her beside the hut where the playthings are stored. It is quite a good little place. You can be almost hidden there. It's private. She has used the spot before to hang out till last minute at the end of playtime.

Emma is there. And Amanda. And, oh no! Anna also spots Georgie in the little group. Georgie, the gossip queen, who's always in a group of girls telling tales about others. Anna is horrified, surely not Emma? She has never gone in for that kind of thing, she's always kept away from the ganging up on someone.

Anna jumps down from the bar. She has decided to go and find out what is going on.

How strange. As soon as Anna starts approaching the small group, they all turn round so that she can only see their backs. They hold their hands over their mouths and whisper into each other's ears. Turn their heads. Look at her and burst into fake little giggles.

When she is really close they all go silent, look at each other and back at her.

Looking her up and down, Georgie turns round to her and asks: "Anything you want?" There's a small pause and then: "Otherwise, I suggest you better get lost. We are playing something you need brains for. Not for you, of course. So get lost."

They all look at each other and giggle again.

Anna feels really bad. That is just so nasty. She feels as if they are actually trying to make her angry. Are they trying to get her into trouble?

Georgie is moving closer to Anna, her head slightly tilted. She is looking directly into her face and says in a nasty voice: "Are you deaf as well as dumb? Push off. Hear me?"

Anna's stomach churns. Some heat is starting to burn around the edges of her ears. She's angry and hurt. Tears are welling up. Her hands are moving up slowly, forming into fists.

She is a lot stronger then stupid Georgie, who smiles a sly grin at Anna, sure of getting her into the right sort of trouble.

Anna's hands go to her pockets. Yes, she still has the dried up cream on the shrivelled leaf, but will it still work?

Not the Queen for me, please!

Suddenly, she gives a laugh and says: "Hey, cool it, guys. Just came over to say 'hi'. See how you all were. But never mind, I know when I am not welcome." She turns, pretending not to mind, to go somewhere else.

Even though her feelings were so hurt, she is strangely happy. She had seen the danger. Spotted it. Dealt with it. And succeeded. The Queen had no chance of getting her. Wow. She starts feeling so good that she is skipping.

"What's wrong with her?" Georgie shouts, really frustrated. She really had looked forward so much to getting Anna into trouble. OK, maybe she would have had a punch or two. But there were three of them and it would have been worth the price.

Georgie had worked hard to get Emma into her clique. Not that she actually liked her that much. She thought Emma was far too nice to others, friendly and kind of naïve. Unlike herself and Amanda. They were clever. But Emma was Anna's best friend, so she was worth having, just to take her away from Anna. Deep down she wanted Anna in her group. She would never admit this even to herself, but secretly she admired her because she was so sporty and always had brilliant ideas of what to do next.

In a nasty shrill voice she tells the others: "Obviously scared of us, haha."

Emma feels a cold shudder go down her back. That was so disgusting. She had seen how Georgie had tried to make Anna fight.

She actually did not really like her. Why had she started hanging out with those two? Amanda was clever and great at school, always very proper, spotless.

But Georgie? No, there was not much worth finding out about her. She was very nasty all the time about others.

Emma discovered that she was getting quite bored with her new friends. All that girly talk. She began to miss Anna's company, who had so many great ideas. You were never able to get bored with her.

Anna is still skipping when she spots Eliza sitting on the 'quiet bench'.

She has a pack of cards she keeps looking at.

She asks with a friendly smile: "Hey, Anna, fancy a game?"

Anna stops. She has never been that keen on card games really. But then again, "Why not try," she thinks to herself.

She jumps onto the bench, where she sits with both her legs tucked under her bum. "Tell me how it goes."

"It is quite easy peasy. Just like pairs. But with a difference. I made it myself. I mean the cards."

Anna nearly stops breathing when she looks at the pictures. There are drawings, drawings of little creatures only she and Philip had seen before. Ants, moles, owls, spiders, toads and – chestnut men! That can't be true!

She looks at Eliza's face with an expression that looks like a question mark.

The girl laughs in a warm way and explains: "You did know you were recommended, didn't you?"

"By the way, loser is the one who is left with the nasty Queen card, haha."

It is great fun. They take turns in losing. They love sharing a precious secret.

"Eliza, I cannot imagine that you ever had an encounter with that horrible Queen? You are always so quiet and friendly? Did you?"

Eliza looks back at Anna and replies: "I did. But not the way you did when you got angry and nasty. I am not like that. I did other things. I don't take it out on kids, more on my mum with words and on things. I did really bad things, like throw my grandma's old doll against the wall. The head broke. And my mum was so sad, because it had been her mum's dolly and with her being dead, that was pretty bad. It was only because of Maths, and you know, with all my difficulties, I was so fed up. But there you go, can't change it. Good thing is I met Mrs Toad, went to owl's school and now the numbers are sorted in my head. It is sooo good, isn't it?"

They play and chat till the bell rings. How quick the break time finishes! Anna had never thought that Eliza was such a nice, interesting girl and they had so much in common.

PHILIP'S CURE

Philip has had a wonderful day at his house. He had been too weak to be able to go to school, so Mum had decided to spoil him and even allow some daytime cartoons on TV. His sister became nearly green with envy when she came home.

At bedtime his mum and dad both tuck his little sister into bed before they come into his room. For the first time in ages, he has been taking books from his shelves, wondering if there is anything he might like to read. There was the 'Giant Peach', hilariously funny. And quite weird, he thought, just like entering a different world down a rainbow spiral, he chuckled to himself.

"You look happy, Philip?" His Dad looks a little bit embarrassed as he sits down on the edge of his bed. He straightens the duvet cover with one hand several times before he continues: "We had a chat, Philip, your mum and I. You know, eh, about what had happened the other evening? I don't really know how to put, but, you know, oh dear. I am, yeah, Philip, I really am sorry. I, I don't know why, but..." Before he can stutter on, his son interrupts: "You just flipped, Dad. Come on Dad, I was a pain in the neck! I deserved it. Well, some of it, anyway."

"No son, I don't think you did. Nobody does. Not like that. It's me. I did not control my temper. I should be able to."

Now his face is really red. Philip's mum looks at both her 'boys'. She has some tears in the corner of her eyes: "I wish you both would just stop in time. Before the anger becomes too strong!"

The three of them agree: they are going to try. Try to have a nicer way with each other. His Dad would have loved to ask Philip if he had forgiven him. But he didn't dare, in case the boy had said: 'No.'

Mum had given him a long cuddle and a kiss. It had been one of the best days for ages for Philip.

At his request, his Dad opens the bedroom window a bit and they close the door behind them when they leave him tucked in.

In no time at all, he drops off into a deep sleep.

He never notices the flapping of the bat's wings as it flies into his bedroom. It circles right round the sleeping child and a weird sheen appears when it sprinkles some powdery substance over the bed.

Philip's body shrinks down to the same size it was when he rode down the spiral before. Next, the bat gently picks him up with its legs and holds him tightly like a mother carrying a baby whilst flying off into the beautiful moonlit night.

They fly over the soft yellow streetlights into the darker space of the park. The echo of the high-pitched scream guides the bat along its way directly to the big old tree, Isolde Owl's institute. They fly straight into the cosy room with the little hammocks. For a very brief moment, Philip opens his eyes and looks around, not even half awake. He just glimpses the shadow of the bat before it flies off.

It is very dark, so he cannot see that some other hammocks are occupied by children of varying ages and sizes. As if moved by invisible hands, the hammocks rock gently from side to side.

His cheek barely touches the unusual material of the cushion and the little blanket, snugly tucked around him by the bat, when he spirals into an unusual dream. All around him he sees sparkles in the most beautiful colours. He feels as if he is floating in the sky and sees his parents and sister also floating. They are all waving and looking happy. He has a very intense feeling of love and being loved. It is incredible.

He does not notice the owl, gently stroking his face with one of her long wing feathers. He does not hear her as she whispers into his ear something about being strong and never giving in to the horrible Queen's spells of anger again. Woody Woodborer is walking around the sleeping kids. He is carrying a bundle of herbs, which are giving off a really lovely smell. Mrs Owl bends forward and whispers to Woody: "Look at him. I think he must be almost cured already. I think there have been some magic changes at home for him. Otherwise, he would not have recovered so quickly. Isn't it just great, Woody?"

Then she flies off onto her nightly rounds, leaving Woody to watch over the dreaming children.

The lining of the hammocks is made from cocoons that normally help to develop butterflies when they change from their caterpillar phase. Now they help the children. They learn to be positive and to feel love.

After a couple of hours, the sky changes from the clear deep blue dark of the night to a warmer golden and turquoise shade, and outside the first few notes of the song of a blackbird are heard. This is the moment the bats come back. They pick the children gently out of the hammocks and fly them home to their own beds. Some of the fluff of the soft cocoons that sticks to their hair is carried back with them.

Straight after being dropped gently onto his bed, Philip's body stretches back to its normal size. He yawns in his sleep, pulls his blanket back over him and turns over.

The magic of the shrinking powder has worn off just at the right time. But the magic of the cure in Isolde Owl's institute will stay with him forever.

MORE FAVOURS

Anna is so much happier at school these days. Everybody notices. She has written a story in class that her teacher says is excellent. Anna reads it to the other children and it is the first time she has read aloud without it being a complete disaster. The story was a scary adventure she had made up. Two kids in their tree house watch some robbers stealing the neighbour's dog. They manage to rescue the dog and help the police catch the villains. She really got so much into her story that she did not notice that everyone in class was glued to her lips as she was reading.

She is still hot with excitement when she has finished. "That was the best story ever," a boy who is normally very nasty to her looks at her in amazement. "Is that something from telly? Must be a film you've seen, Anna?" he asks her. She shakes her head. "No, just a story I made up."

Her classmates are all amazed. "That should be made into a film then," one of them says. Anna has never felt so good about anything she had done in school before. She feels like floating on a cloud.

So Anna comes down with a bump from the sky, when she realises that she still can't do her Maths, especially her tables.

The awful Queen had shown her nasty face briefly from behind the classroom's computer screen and tried to lure Anna back into one of her old angry fits when she just could not get to the next level of her exercises, but Anna would not give in.

She was so bored with the seven times table as there were no earworms to help her along with it.

"Stupid, stupid numbers. I hate you," came a scream inside her head. But as soon as she felt the tiniest bit of the tentacle's heat, Anna had managed to calm down enough to make the Queen disappear.

At least she had learned that!

"Anna, go back to Mrs Owl!" Eliza says to her in the playground. "Look how much she helped me with Maths."

"But I feel so embarrassed about all that carry on with Philip. I caused it, you know," she explains to her friend. She has told her the whole story, and it felt great to safely talk about it all without revealing her secret to the wrong person.

"Down there they understand. They'll be great. Just go. I am sure they'll help you again. They want you to be happy. Stay one of us. Not be a victim of the Queen again."

She continues: "Look, I am not scared of any numbers anymore. I learned it with the rainbows. It was so much fun and so easy! Go Anna, go."

Later, she sees Philip. He looks so different. His face has lost the angry folds between the eyebrows and he smiles a lot. He tells Anna of his nightly adventure, his flight with the bat mobile, and the dreams. He also explains how his parents are really nice to him at the moment. He still fights a bit with his sister, but not in a nasty way. Only for fun. Teasing. Anna tells him about her Maths and how she would love to improve it.

"So would I," he admits to her. "Shall we ask to be allowed to go back? I can now cry the right kind of tears. Not the angry ones."

They look at each other and say at the same time: "Let's ride a rainbow then!" There hands come up immediately, clapping together to give 'fives'! They burst into a fit of giggles.

In the meantime, Otto is sitting in Mrs Toad's place. They both are very busy. The late summer has produced a bumper harvest of the juiciest blackberries. Like the mushrooms, they need to be threaded up and hung over the stove for drying, so they'll have lovely dried fruit, just like raisins, for the coming winter. Everyone has helped with the gathering and storing. There is a wasteland on the other side of the river. The ants have done a fantastic job of transporting the big berries across the high arch of the bridge down to the entrance of the hollow. It's meant lots and lots of tiring long trips forward and back.

The trips are dangerous too as all those big feet are their enemies. People do not see them or even worse, some deliberately stamp on the tiny creatures carrying the massive loads, which are often bigger than they are.

So they try to work mainly when the park is empty. But the daytime is now getting shorter and shorter.

One storage area is filled already with dry nettle leaves. They make such a nice and healthy soup. Otto loves thinking of his food. He is looking forward to the cosy days of winter when daylight is in short supply, and the air in the early morning and evening is filled with the cold breath of fog that rises and floats from the nearby river.

It is the time when the park gets busy with fairies and friendly ghosts; fun loving trolls playing little tricks to entertain everyone.

Lots of visitors gather in the hollow to warm themselves in the yellow glow of Mrs Toad's stove. Sitting together, they sip sap teas, nibble on bits of dried berry, surrounded by the gorgeous scent of a mushroom stew gently simmering on the top. It smells of wild marjoram, pine needles and other flavours that are added to the pot. They tell each other stories.

They all have a busy time in the summer and early autumn preparing for the winter. So it is a well-deserved time of rest.

They never get bored. There are so many games, so many stories. They have a special collection of leaves, very similar to each other. They play 'snap' with it. They know a huge number of different games to play with little round pebbles, which they use in a similar way to marbles. The crickets are there to entertain them with their music.

They are also busy making things. They tear the cocoons that the butterflies have left into strips to be woven into cushions and blankets. The long strands of fibre from the stems of nettles are knitted or woven into material for clothes and they use different colourings to decorate them from rose petals, autumn leaves, some earth or ground up stones.

Otto's clothes are usually made by the tiny money spiders. That's why they are so fine. He is very careful about his looks. While threading another berry, he secretly looks at his favourite red boots. He was so chuffed when he got them. They were made from a bit of plastic taken from a good quality shopping bag that some person had carelessly thrown away. One of his cousins is a shoemaker who made these beautiful boots for him and a few others.

Toady and Otto are chatting about the recent events. They talk about Anna and Philip.

"I have the feeling that our mission with Anna is almost finished. She has been such a fast learner.

Nothing to get soppy about, old toad, I tell myself. Sad to see them go. But it is just so good for them when they can't cry the sorrows of the world anymore. And Philip. Well, I think he might need a little help with his learning, but now the Queen can't take his energy so much. Well, what do you think, dear old friend?"

She turns her face towards Otto, looking into his eyes through her enormous glasses.

"Och I, deary. I think you are quite right. Nice to see our little customers not needing us anymore. Wonder who the lad will recommend to us?"

"Yes, it'll be interesting who he will chose to become one of us." The toad looks dreamingly into the flames of the fire. "Guess it's best if he waits for the next spring. Easier on the transport front."

"Aye, hope he does not send someone as challenging as he was. Bringing the Queen down and so," Otto sighs.

"Oh yes, must reinforce the rules a bit. Not sharing a tear ever again, please. Wow, I was impressed by everyone. We did stand up to her properly. So much good team work there. Rat is just so clever." She turns her head round suddenly saying: "Did you hear that? Is there someone?"

There is a very gentle quiet knock on the door. Otto, who sits closer to the entrance, gets up with a sigh, saying: "Dear, dear. Them old bone," and waddles with stiff legs to open it.

"Talking of the devil! Sorry, not the devil, figure of speech if you get what I mean," he blushes to a deep chestnut red. "I mean we just spoke of you two. Aye, Mrs Toad, we have visitors."

Anna and Philip walk in, looking a bit embarrassed.

"Hello, Mrs Toad. Hello Otto. We hope you don't mind us just dropping in again?"

"Welcome you two," the friendly smile of the old toad says it all. "No not at all. As a matter of fact, we have just been talking about you."

Anna and Philip look at each other and Philip says: "Oh no. Hope it's not about all the problems I have caused?"

Otto laughs: "No, come on. What has happened happened. Only thing is, we all need to learn from it. Otherwise, just forget it. Ended well. Nice concert as well. Need to have a gig organised sometime. Just for fun. Old feller, Green Man will love it."

Mrs Toad adds: "If you managed to cry some tears of sorrow it shows that your program was not quite finished, Anna. And you, Philip, might benefit from a bit of Isolde's teaching too?"

She looks at both kids and continues: "So tell me, what is on your mind. Let's organise the next bit."

"It is so embarrassing, Mrs Toad, but you all are just so generous. I don't know how to thank you?"

"Don't be silly, children. We love to help. Anyway, we now have two more people who will treat us and our environment with more respect. Not kicking mushrooms over for no reason. Not trampling on insects and so on. That is the good that comes out for us. You'll tell others to be nicer. You'll help us more than you think."

"Of course, we will. That is the least we can do." Both children look very serious as they promise.

Philip's face has blushed to a deep crimson red. He stutters: "Oh dear, eh, hm. I don't know what to say. But I feel so bad. I have, you know, well. Oh Otto, I hope I have not kicked one of your houses. I am so, so sorry."

"Well Philip. We did know who you were. First, there was no way we wanted you down here. But then, it was Anna's choice. And we did know you needed us. So we took the risk. And, mmh, no point in looking back."

Otto shakes his head gently.

"Oh lad. Not to worry anymore. I am quite used to rebuilding every now and then. A bit of a nuisance, but as long as I manage to get myself out before, you know... Sure you'll never do that again, eh?"

"No, of course not. And I am happy to help you any time you need me. Just let me know. I am quite strong, you know?" Philip's face looks a bit more relaxed.

"That's good of you. Hope it will not come to that, mind. But thanks anyhow!"

Mrs Toad nods and turns her attention back to both children: "Now, let us know what we can do for you."

"Mrs Toad, do you remember a girl called Eliza?" Anna asks.

"Yes, of course. Lovely girl. Has some big problems poor thing. But we did the best we could for her. She'll cope with the rest. Strong little mind she has."

Anna tells her: "She is now my best friend. I would have never found you without her, I know now. She is so nice and I can help her with some things that she finds difficult. She said that I should ask for help for us in Maths. It worked so well with her. Could you...?"

"That will be easy to arrange. Both of you?" She looks at them.

They nod and say: "Yes, please, if it is possible."

"Come back the day after it has rained the next time. Isolde Owl will be ready for you then."

They both look forward to this next teaching of the unusual owl and riding back in the rainbow spiral is superb fun again.

RAIN

This year is an exceptional one. Instead of damp grey autumn days, there seems to be a never-ending row of fine very sunny days. It is nearly November, but people are still talking of an Indian summer.

It is great in the playground. Lots of leaves have fallen down off the trees. Anna and Eliza are playing together all the time. They have been making 'houses'. They gather the leaves by pushing them with their feet and piling them up into little walls that surround the different rooms of their houses. They clear the floor areas with little broken off branches they have found, using them as brushes. They both have houses side by side so they can visit each other.

"I wish we really were neighbours," says Eliza longingly. "We could play in each other's gardens."

"Yes that would be so cool, we could make a hole in the fence and make it one big garden."

They are totally immersed into their play world and do not notice the girl standing on the side watching them with longing eyes. It is Emma. She would so much love to join in. It is just the sort of play Emma misses since she's stopped playing with Anna.

Would Anna forgive her? Will they let her in?

But she does not get a chance. Just as she takes a deep breath to ask the two girls the difficult question, Georgie appears from behind her, hooks an arm under her elbow and whooshes her away. She says in a nasty voice: "Just look at those two babies! Make believe play! Haha. That is just soooo childish!"

She looks at Emma and tells her in a very loud voice: "Come and chat with us. We are planning a makeup party. Maybe with a sleepover. You know: Real makeup!"

Emma does not know what to do, but puts on her best false smile and joins in the 'grown-up' chat with Georgie and Amanda.

In the meantime, the other two have paid no attention to what has gone on.

"We have a chestnut tree in our garden. Let's bring in some toothpicks and I will collect lots of conkers. I can probably find some acorns as well for the heads, then we can make some chestnut men and pretend. Look over there, under the tree, there is a lovely little hollow!"

"Oh yeah, let's make some clothes and furniture for them as well. I'll bring things for that."

The girls giggle excitedly. They are looking forward to their plan.

In the meantime, Emma keeps looking over to them. She would love to be part of their play. She is bored by the other two's talk about lipstick and nail varnish!

However, they do not get a chance to make their own little hollow under the tree. For when they wake up in the morning, the rain is pouring down from the sky as if buckets were being emptied out.

Indoor playtime is usually quite a boring affair, made up of reading, watching a very old film on a screen or just hanging around. Nobody really likes it much.

But Anna and Eliza dig out the things they have brought in and instead of making the little chestnut figures outside, they make them at their desks. In a way, it is easier as they have scissors and paper readily available. It is quite hard to pierce little holes in the big fat conker to stick the toothpicks in to form the arms and legs. But after a lot of broken toothpicks, they achieve quite good results. They find bits of playdough and form little welly boots so that the figures can stand up. They look really sweet and funny. Emma has decided that this is definitively superb play, so she takes the courage to ask whether she can make one as well.

"Yes, of course," is the prompt answer. Both girls speak at exactly the same moment. "Snap!" they laugh.

Others decide that this is 'cool'. So, in no time, at all the classroom starts to be filled with quite a sizeable chestnut people population.

They make houses and furniture from paper and some loo rolls. Everything gets decorated in the most gorgeous way. One of the houses has a fully laid table, with knifes and forks and everything! Anna is decorating a mini kitchen with paper mushrooms. She has made a stove and painted the flames, and a tiny little kettle with a whistle that looks like a face! Even some of the boys join in. Some of them make castles rather than houses.

At the end of playtime the class teacher enters. She at first thinks something is wrong because they are all so quiet. But when she sees the little fantasy world they have made, she exclaims: "Wow, this is so beautiful. I can't believe you made all this. We must keep this somewhere. Careful, when you're moving it!"

"Pooh. Rubbish! Just a pile of paper, some old conkers and garbage," sniggers Georgie, green with envy.

She kicks one of the little men Anna has made. It falls apart. "See!" She grins a nasty smile. "Just as I said."

Anna picks up the pieces, puts them together and whispers: "Empty-headed."

Only Eliza hears. She grins and nods towards her friend.

During lesson time, Anna watches the rain form little rivulets on the windows outside. She is happy. Tomorrow. Tomorrow she will return to the real creatures. The day after the rain!

Philip is very happy too. On his way home, he keeps jumping into the puddles on the pavement causing superb splashes whilst whistling a happy tune.

RAINBOW NUMBERS

Otto knows that today the two children will be coming, so he is waiting for them by the window of his little cottage. It has stopped raining, but it is still very damp and quite cold outside.

He has arranged for Rupert the mole to be on standby for transport.

"This might be the last visit," he thinks. "Just in time before the winter."

Next thing he hears is the soft plop of one of the children landing, followed by another plop as the other one arrives.

They brush off their trousers and laugh when they see a little wet figure of eight on both their bums from the soaking moss.

The three friends greet each other with huge hugs. And in no time at all, Rupert appears out of a molehill next to them. He had heard their plops, and has to clean his glasses as the soil is so muddy it sticks to them.

He takes the children down the tube after telling them that Isy is waiting for them.

When they arrive, they have a lot of brushing to do to get the mud of their clothes.

"Never mind," they laugh.

Woody Woodborer leads them into the games room this time.

The old owl is standing in the far corner. She hugs them both to her feathery chest. One of the soft down feathers tickles Anna's nose so that she has to sneeze.

"Bless you, my dear. But come and sit on this mat, the two of you." The teacher shows them a very comfortable floormat. Then she goes and pushes two colourful boxes over to them.

"Go on, open them," she invites them.

The children take off the lids and gasp as the whole room is suddenly filled with an amazing shine.

The boxes are filled with rods, all in a neat row, according to their size, one beside the other. Each glows a wonderful colour. They are not solid looking, but rather like colourful glass that is sort of semi see-through.

Anna and Philip are speechless. They have never ever seen anything as beautiful as these rods.

They dare not touch, in case they'll vanish.

"Go on feel them. Take them out. Play." The owl smiles at the children. "They won't break. They are pieces of a rainbow. Quite solid, you know. Go on, see what they do for you!"

Anna glances over to Philip. Does he have the same sensation when he touches them? She can't really describe hers. Are the pieces of rainbow warm, hot or cold?

Are they heavy or light? Weird. They seem to be almost alive. They make her put them in a certain order.

Anna shouts: "Like a puzzle. A rainbow puzzle!"

Philip has put his upright in a row and shouts excitedly: "A rainbow stair. It is a stair!"

"Climb up then, Philip. Climb up!" Isy Owl knew these children were bright.

As Philip climbs on the different colours, he hears numbers being called out in his head. From sort of inside it. This is a very gentle and pleasant sound, like little bells at Christmas.

He shouts as he jumps from colour to colour: "This is so much fun!"

Anna quickly puts hers upright in the same way, starting with the longest and picking up the last one of Philip's. Now they have a perfect rainbow to climb on.

Isy Owl tells them to find certain numbers. Sure enough, in no time at all, they are able to find them just from their colour. The owl now gives them sums to do. They master them in no time at all.

"I can see the numbers in my head. They are beautiful! They show themselves to me." Anna is very excited. She loves this type of Maths.

"More, More. More difficult, please!" she begs.

Philip is the same. He can't believe that learning can be fun.

It is more like an exercise class. Jumping over numbers, adding and multiplying, while the numbers of the times tables are visible in their heads. There's no problem remembering the odd one!

The owl watches. She has given them quite complicated tasks already, so she knows now they are masters of numbers.

"I am getting tired, children. It is time to stop the class. We must make sure the rainbow pieces don't lose their shine on you," she explains.

"That way the shine will last forever inside your heads. You will never have to be frightened of numbers again. You'll see them, all of the colourful combinations."

Woody has reappeared at the back of the class, ready to take them down. But before that, he offers them a little refreshment from his sap tea collection.

Anna and Philip are so happy. They feel like their hearts will burst. It is so lovely here. All the shine of the rainbows and then the incredible flavour of the tea! They wish this moment would last forever.

But Rupert the mole is waiting.

They bid their farewells. Woody's hug is really 'woody'. It almost creeks!

Isy Owl secretly wipes a tear from the corner of her eye. She loves them so much, but her mission is fulfilled.

She waves from the hole in the tree trunk just before the kids disappear behind Rupert down into the tube.

She is thinking: "Look at this boy. How he's turned out in the end. After all that trouble, he is great!"

She sighs, she can't see them any longer.

SUCCESS

Anna is praised in class by her teacher. She has done the whole set of her maths in record time.

"Well done, Anna. I am impressed!" Her teacher looks at her in a questioning way. "Just shows you, hey. I have told you how to do it over and over again. Finally, it clicked. I am glad I did not give up."

She knows she is such a good teacher who knows just how to explain it, after doing her job for so many years. She strokes a lock of her curly hair out of her face and stands up straight, very proudly.

Eliza gives Anna a secret little wink and a smile. They both know who they have to thank for making Maths so easy. But never mind. Let her be.

The teacher's moment of glory is soon over. Eddy, who has been tilting his chair backwards too far, loses balance and crashes to the ground with an almighty bang.

He does not cry or show that he's banged his head. Instead, Eddy jumps back up and gathers up all the worksheets, pencils, eraser and a lot of other paraphernalia that has gone down with him. He stands his chair back upright and apologises, looking as red as a beetroot: "Sorry, so sorry..." But before he is able to finish even that, the sound of the teacher screaming at him comes down on him like thunder.

"I have told you so often, for goodness sake. Are you deaf? You, you... I know I am not allowed to say what I think you are. But you are!"

And so on and on...

'Here we go. The dragon is spitting its fire again,' thinks Anna, knowing the teacher too well.

She never shows any love for her job and is only ever kind to certain children, like Georgie, Amanda and a few others.

Still, Anna is enjoying doing her Maths work. She has been given more and more sheets, finishing them in record time.

She just looks at the numbers and they appear in rainbow colours right in her head. Magic. They move around as they join up with each other, change colours and get larger or smaller, just as required. And then, well, she just 'sees' what she should write down. It is amazing. She wishes she was allowed to use coloured pencils to write them in. That would look so much nicer.

Because she is so quick, her teacher runs out of worksheets for her and she is allowed to do some of the learning games, reserved normally for the fastest and brightest, for the first time in her life.

Anna feels as if she is sitting on a cloud, or even better on a rainbow above the class.

In Philip's class, some similar events are taking place.

Philip finishes every sheet his Maths teacher hands to him in no time at all. At first, his teacher pays him no attention. But after the third sheet in probably as many minutes, he looks at the boy in a strange way. He hands him the next sheet and watches him, but can't find out how the boy manages them. Does his neighbour help him?

"Max McIntyre, pack your things and sit on this desk!" his teacher says, thinking himself clever by removing the suspect helper.

"But why, Sir? What have I done?" asks the innocent child.

"Just do as you're told. I have my reasons, but I have no intention of telling you, young man!" The teacher is still not sure of how Philip is cheating, but now he has a clearer view. 'Where is that boy hiding the calculator?'

"Philip stand up, shake your jumper. You are not going to deceive me! Been around for a long time, seen it all, boy." But nothing drops out of the large school jumper.

The teacher gets all flustered. Now he is searching Philip's desk and his schoolbag. He even tells him to turn his pockets inside out.

"OK, young man, sit at my desk, then we'll see," he says sniggering as he gives him a new sheet.

He now only has eyes for what Philip is doing. The rest of the class only has eyes for Philip. The teacher does not notice they have stopped working.

He completes sheet after sheet, graded to become more and more difficult, with great ease.

Philip feels happy. It is the first time he's ever felt like that in school. He finds it quite funny to watch the teacher. He does not blame him for the accusation of cheating. He would normally have done so, but this was so easy! Maths was just so easy! Rainbow bit fitted together with rainbow bit, then changed size and colour, and became bigger or smaller, depending on the task. It was fun, fun, so much fun! All those colours. He remembers jumping up and down the rainbows with Anna. How was she getting on?

It felt good, so relaxed not to be in the power of the Queen. Not to get angry about silly numbers tumbling up and down the pages.

"How strange, what is going on?" the teacher wonders to himself.

"This is not the normal Philip. Far too calm and sensible, strange indeed."

He gives him more and more worksheets but thinks: 'Let's enjoy it while it lasts. He will soon be himself again...'

But before he runs out of prepared work for the boy, he sits Philip at the computer and lets him do some educational game.

Max, who had been removed from the seat next to him earlier, asks Philip at the end of the period, as they are leaving for playtime:

"You want to join us for football? We could do with you in our team, please?" Strange things were happening. Philip had never been popular before. He was famous for not fitting in with teams.

Philip feels even better. He has never let on that it hurt him not to be asked, not to have friends.

His mother looks at him in astonishment when he comes in from school and tells her about his day: "Maths is just so easy, Mum. I caught up so much today. And you know Mum, maybe I can stay in class now. I would love it so much. Max said he liked my defence shot, when I prevented a goal. And Mum, can I join the under-twelves on Saturdays? Please, Mum? And what's for dinner, I am hungry? And, Mum, can you help me cut my nails. I think they are revolting."

His mum's head is spinning with this bombardment of things. She has not heard this kind of happy chatter from him for a long time. 'Is it the diet change? Maybe he did have too much sugar before. He is so different.' It is great and she feels so light, as if a big stone has been removed from her chest. She looks at her big boy with very proud eyes.

She gives him a big hug and a kiss, he might be big, but he's still her boy. He grins and does not mind at all. Nobody saw it anyway.

"Love ye too," he says when she tells him she does.

Anna's parents are impressed when she tells them about her Maths. "Haha, tables, come on, ask me a question, easy peasy, japaneesy."

"Go on then: What's eight sevens?" That, of course, is her sister asking, knowing this is one of the most difficult ones. Anna just grins, enjoying the dancing rainbows: "Fifty six, of course, haha." She is skipping through the kitchen chanting: "Nine times seven is sixty three, ten times seven seventy!"

"She is really good at story writing as well, now. I met her form teacher while shopping the other day. She said Anna has caught up a lot. She has this really good teacher at lunchtime. Finally! I think we need to write her a 'Thank you' note and send her something nice as well, what do you think?" Her Mum looks at her Dad. They both look proud and pleased about their younger daughter's achievements.

Anna does not tell them the 'real' story. It is a secret, even from her parents. Her sister has left the kitchen. She is not sure of what to think of the praise her little sister is suddenly getting.

Later, Philip is very generous to his sister and let's her have a go on the Wii, his favourite gadget. It was a Christmas present to both, but normally acquired by him.

Instead of the electronic play, Philip digs out his long abandoned colouring pens and a large sheet of paper. He is making a big picture to put above his bed. He makes the background a deep night blue, crossed by a massive big rainbow with an owl flying below it.

"What is that? asks his father. "Wow, that owl looks so real, Philip. I did not know you could draw like that. That just looks stunning! You should do more. You never know, you might have talent. By the way, Mum says you've made progress in Maths. That is just so good. I am chuffed. Hey boy, I meant to ask you, can we forget some of the things that's happened? Sort of start afresh?" Philip looks at his father in astonishment. He is asking him? He grins in embarrassment. "Gimmie five!" They both laugh because they have said it at the same time, as they clap their hands together for a high and low five.

In the evening, after Philip has gone to bed, he thinks back to all of the exciting events. He is so grateful to Anna. He feels good. He has new friends. And he is one of 'them'. There are now three of the Chosen' in school who know of each other. Are there more?

He knows he is supposed to recommend the next child for treatment down the rainbow and feels very responsible. He has to judge who needs to go, but also if they can be trusted not to let in the wicked Queen of Fury and all the evil she brings with her. There is no rush. Best to do it after the winter, like they told him, so he has some time to decide.

He feels very cosy when he snuggles himself in under his duvet. He looks again at the owl on his painting and turns off the light.

The End

ACKNOWLEDGEMENT

Writing this book would have been impossible without the inspiration and motivation that I have gained from some amazing children or the support and encouragement from my family and Marcus Ferrar (Author) who so kindly helped me edit it!

ABOUT THE AUTHOR

Stefanie was born and brought up in Düsseldorf, where she lived for many years.

She has always been captivated by children. Being a very creative person, she was able to engage with them in a way that absorbed and inspired them, constantly helping them to learn through creative experience and imaginative storytelling. As a result of this passion for children, she studied to become a primary teacher at Düsseldorf University, graduating as one of the top students in her year at Teacher Training College. Stefanie has a great talent in engaging with children through many different media.

Stefanie moved to Scotland to get married, ultimately moving to Oxford, where she established her home. As a keen linguist, she took this all in her stride and brought up her two children to be bilingual. Being married to a dyslexic and having a daughter who also suffered from dyslexia, she became fascinated by the way the brain works and the way in which people with learning difficulties cope with their challenges. Stefanie decided to specialise in this area, training to become a Special Educational Needs Teacher in a multilingual school. Bringing this together with her inspiring, creative and engaging approach to teaching, she had the opportunity to gain a deep insight into the challenges faced by these children and also their parents. Her students love her and she has a great ability to draw out their strengths and help them develop techniques to overcome their difficulties, building up their confidence and ability to learn.

The combination of her great insight into child development and her creativity enabled her to draw huge inspiration from the children under her guidance. They inspired her and she inspired them, and this led to the development of Anna's story.

Stefanie wrote this book to help children with learning difficulties to understand that they are special, they are not alone, and can be confident in learning their way. Equally, she wrote it in a way to help parents relate to the challenges that they encounter with children who struggle with learning.

Now semi-retired, Stefanie maintains her interest in child development and has developed as an artist, producing the imaginative illustrations in this book.

www.ingramcontent.com/pod-product-compliance
Lightning Source LLC
Chambersburg PA
CBHW031110080526
44587CB00011B/912